ELECTRONIC PROJECTS
FOR BEGINNERS

by

R. A. PENFOLD

BERNARD BABANI (publishing) LTD
THE GRAMPIANS
SHEPHERDS BUSH ROAD
LONDON W6 7NF
ENGLAND

PLEASE NOTE

Although every care has been taken with the production of this book to ensure that any projects, designs, modifications and/or programs, etc., contained herewith, operate in a correct and safe manner and also that any components specified are normally available in Great Britain, the Publishers and Author do not accept responsibility in any way for the failure, including fault in design, of any project, design, modification, or program to work correctly or to cause damage to any other equipment that it may be connected to or used in conjunction with, or in respect of any other damage or injury that may be caused, nor do the Publishers accept responsibility in any way for the failure to obtain specified components.

Notice is also given that if equipment that is still under warranty is modified in any way or used or connected with home-built equipment then that warranty may be void.

© 1996 BERNARD BABANI (publishing) LTD

First Published – January 1996
Reprinted August 2003
Reprinted May 2004
Reprinted June 2005

British Library Cataloguing in Publication Data

A catalogue record for this book is available from the British Library

ISBN 0 85934 392 8

Printed and bound in Great Britain by Cox & Wyman Ltd, Reading

Preface

Although we live in a world that is virtually saturated with electronic gadgets, electronics still retains a certain mystique. This is probably due to the fact that electronic devices often provide complex functions, but they have no mechanisms that can be seen to be working away to make the gadgets work. Electronic circuits can perform extremely complex tasks at amazing speeds, but there is no outward sign of anything at all happening on the circuit board.

This lack of cogs, shafts, and other moving parts tends to put off many would-be electronic project constructors. Building your own electronic gadgets looks very daunting, with all those unfamiliar components and construction methods. Also, it means building something when you have no real idea of how it works. In reality, the fascinating hobby of electronics is something that can be undertaken by anyone who is reasonably intelligent and not totally useless at manual tasks. You do not need to be particularly good at electronics theory in order to build projects. Indeed, you do not need to understand any electronics theory in order to build electronic gadgets, and the hobby can be pursued as a form of craft.

This book covers the basic facts and skills you will need in order to get started in the engrossing hobby of electronic project construction. Topics covered include components, tools, construction methods, and simple fault-finding. It does not tell you everything you will ever need to know – electronics is a hobby where you are always learning something new. However, this book does cover the information you will need in order to get started.

R. A. Penfold

Other Titles of Interest

Contents

Chapter 1

COMPONENTS

The hobby of electronic project construction is generally regarded as highly technical, and of more interest to those of an academic rather than a practical disposition. While I would not claim that it is possible to pursue this hobby properly without any technical knowledge at all, it is possible to build simple but useful projects with little or no understanding of electronics theory. In due course most project builders feel the need to learn at least some of the fundamentals of electronics. A knowledge of electronics theory is certainly more than a little useful when the occasional project fails to work first time, but it is not an essential part of the hobby.

However, even if you choose to totally ignore the theoretical side of things, there are still some technical matters that must be tackled if projects are to be constructed properly. The first obstacle for beginners to overcome is the unfamiliarity of the components and materials used. Building furniture, making toys, metalworking, etc., involve what are mainly familiar materials. By contrast, electronics involves the use of resistors, capacitors, integrated circuits, diodes, and so on. These may have been encountered at school or college, but for most beginners at project building they are a new experience.

In this first chapter we will consider component related topics such as identifying components, colour codes, and component values. Much of the information included here is primarily for reference purposes. If you have problems identifying the value of a capacitor or the polarity of a rectifier, the relevant sections of this chapter should tell you what you need to know. Nevertheless, it is a good idea to read through this chapter as it will help with the familiarisation process.

I would also recommend that all beginners obtain at least a couple of component catalogues from mail order component suppliers, and then spend plenty of time looking through them. Most component catalogues contain numerous photographs of components, plus useful data and other information that will help to familiarise you with modern components. Even if you

1

do happen to live close to an electronic component retailer, the range and diversity of current electronic components is such that you will still need to use mail order outlets from time to time. A couple of component catalogues, including at least one of the larger ones, has to be regarded as an essential part of the hobby.

Resistors

Virtually every electronic project uses a number of these, and they are probably used in larger quantities than any other electronic component. Fortunately, they are also very cheap, and even the more exotic types mostly cost no more than a few pence each. Physically a resistor usually looks like a small tubular shaped object with a wire protruding from the centre of each end. The value is normally marked using a system of colour coding, with four or five coloured bands around the body of each component.

Resistor values are in units known as ohms. This unit of measurement is named after Ohm, the German physicist. The abbreviation for the ohm is the Greek letter omega (Ω). This letter gives problems with modern computer based word processors, computer aided drawing programs, etc., and it has to some extent been replaced by the letter R (always in upper case).

An ohm is a small unit of measurement, and practical resistors cover a wide range of values. A component catalogue would typically list values from about 0.1 ohms to about 10 million ohms. Kilohms and megohms are the units used when dealing with very high values. A kilohm is equal to 1000 ohms, and a megohm is equal to 1000 kilohms or 1000000 ohms. A resistor having a value of 2200 ohms would normally have its value written as 2.2 kilohms. This would normally abbreviated to 2.2k (possibly with omega following the "k", but it is often omitted these days). A resistor having a value of 4700000 ohms would normally have its value written as 4.7M. Again, omega might be included at the end of the value, but it is superfluous and is often omitted these days.

On circuit diagrams, and sometimes elsewhere, the unit of measurement is also used to indicate the position of the decimal point. The general idea of this is to reduce the number of

2

digits in values, which helps to keep complex circuit diagrams as uncluttered as possible. Values of 3.3 ohms, 4.7k, and 5.6M would therefore be written as 3R3, 4k7, and 5M6 on circuit diagrams. This method is also used a great deal for components lists.

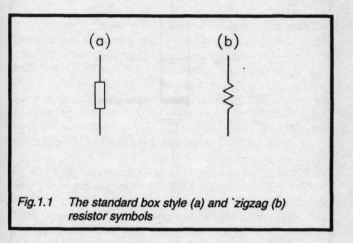

Fig.1.1   The standard box style (a) and `zigzag (b) resistor symbols

The circuit symbol for a resistor is shown in Figure 1.1(a). This is the current British standard, but its "zigzag" predecessor is still in widespread use. The zigzag version is shown in Figure 1.1(b). The box style resistor is the one used in most electronics books (but not all). The zigzag version seems to be the one used by most British electronics magazines.

Figure 1.2 provides basic details of the standard four band method of resistor colour coding. The first two bands indicate the first two digits of the value, and the third band is the multiplier. The first two digits are multiplied by the figure represented by the third band, and this gives the full value of the component. The fourth band indicates the tolerance of the component. This table shows the figures represented by the various colours.

3

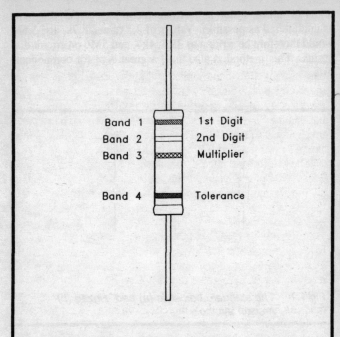

Fig. 1.2   The standard four band resistor colour code

Colour	Band 1	Band 2	Band 3	Band 4
Black	0	0	×1	–
Brown	1	1	×10	1%
Red	2	2	×100	2%
Orange	3	3	×1000	–
Yellow	4	4	×10000	–
Green	5	5	×100000	0.5%
Blue	6	6	×1000000	0.25%
Violet	7	7	–	0.1%
Grey	8	8	–	–
White	9	9	–	–
Gold	–	–	×0.1	5%
Silver	–	–	×0.01	10%
None	–	–	–	20%

4

Thus a resistor having yellow, violet, red, and gold coloured bands has a value of 4700 ohms, or 4.7k (4k7), and its actual value is within +5% of that nominal value. This information is derived in the following manner. As will be seen from the table above, the yellow band indicates that the first digit is four, and the violet one indicates that the second digit is seven. This gives us 47, which then has to be multiplied by the amount indicated by the third band. This band is red, which indicates a multiplier value of 100. The value of the component is therefore 47 × 100, which is clearly 4700 ohms or 4.7k.

The fourth band is gold, which corresponds to a tolerance of ±5%. No resistor has precisely its marked value, and the tolerance marking gives guaranteed limits. In this case the value of the resistor is in the range 4.465k to 4.935k. If a components list specifies a tolerance rating of 5%, it is obviously all right to use a type which has a closer tolerance, such as 1% or 2%. It is not acceptable to use a lesser tolerance than that specified in a components list. For example, if 1% resistors are specified, it would not be acceptable to use 5% types.

In order to correctly decode a value it is clearly necessary to read the bands in the right direction. In most cases there is no problem here, because the fourth band will be either gold (5%) or silver (10%). Neither of these are used for band one. With other tolerances there is scope for confusion, and a little more care has to be taken. In days gone by the first band was closer to its end of the body than the fourth band was to its end. Looking at a selection of modern resistors this does not always seem to be the case any more. The more reliable method is to look at the grouping of the bands. Bands one to three are usually grouped quite closely together, with band four spaced well away from them.

Five Band Codes

The four band method of coding is satisfactory for values in the normal E12 and E24 series of preferred values, but it is unable to accommodate some of the odd values sometimes used in industrial electronics. A five band coding is used for these awkward values, and resistors supplied to amateur users are sometimes marked with these five band codes. Figure 1.3 shows the way in which this method of five band coding

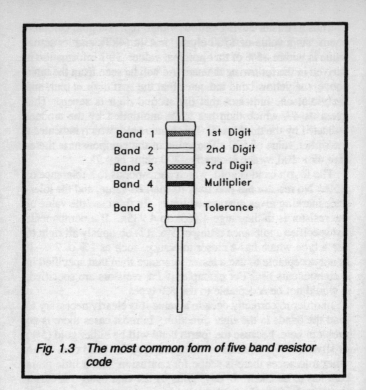

Band 1	1st Digit
Band 2	2nd Digit
Band 3	3rd Digit
Band 4	Multiplier
Band 5	Tolerance

Fig. 1.3   The most common form of five band resistor code

operates, and it has clear similarities with the four band method. In fact the first two and last two bands have the same functions as the bands in the normal four colour system. An extra band is grafted into the middle of the code in order to permit values to be marked more precisely.

If we take a simple example, a coding of red – white – green – red – brown would indicate a value of 29.5k and a tolerance of plus and minus one percent. The first three bands give the first three digits of the value, which in this case are "295". The fourth band is the multiplier, and a red band indicates that the first three digits must be multiplied by 100. This gives a total value of 29500 ohms (295 multiplied by 100 equals 29500), or 29.5k in other words. The fifth band is brown, which indicates a tolerance of plus and minus one percent. Most of these five band resistors have a tolerance of one or two percent.

As component retailers only sell resistors which have normal preferred values, the extra band does not really fulfil any useful purpose as far as amateur users are concerned. Any resistors you buy which use this method of coding will almost certainly have a black third band. For example, a 39k two percent tolerance resistor would have the colour code orange – white – black – red – red. You can therefore calculate the value by ignoring the third band, and using a multiplier ten times higher than indicated by the fourth band.

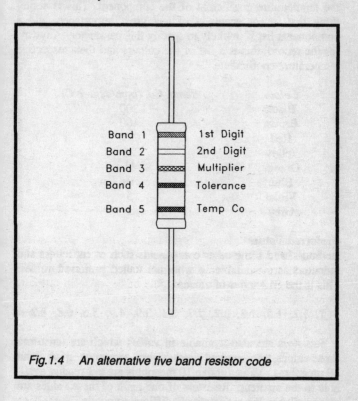

Fig.1.4   An alternative five band resistor code

There is an alternative form of five band resistor code, and details of this code are provided in Figure 1.4. Having two different five band codes is obviously a bit unfortunate, and it is essential to look carefully at any five band code in order to ascertain which particular type it is. If in doubt, the value of the resistor can only be determined for certain by measuring it using a multimeter. Fortunately, in most cases it is fairly obvious which method of coding is in use.

This second five band coding is very straightforward, and is essentially the same as the normal four band variety. The first four bands indicate the value and tolerance rating using the standard four band method of coding. The fifth band indicates the temperature coefficient of the component. This is something that is not normally of any great importance, and a components list is unlikely to specify this parameter. Anyway, for the record, this is a list of the colours and their respective temperature coefficients.

Colour	Temp. Co. (ppm/degree C)
Black	200
Brown	100
Red	50
Yellow	25
Orange	15
Blue	10
Violet	5
Grey	1

Preferred Values

Resistors, and some other components such as capacitors and inductors, are available in what are called preferred values. This is the E12 series of values:

1, 1.2, 1.5, 1.8, 2.2, 2.7, 3.3, 3.9, 4.7, 5.6, 6.8, 8.2

Resistors are also available in values which are ten times these values, one hundred times higher, and so on up to about 10 megohms. Values above 10 megohms are not readily available to the amateur. Resistors of one tenth of these values are also available, but are relatively difficult to obtain.

This system may seem a little unusual to the beginner, but it is really quite logical. If you study the values you will find that each one is about 20% higher than its predecessor. Close tolerance resistors (5% or better) are often available in what are called the E24 series of values. This consists of all the values in the E12 series plus the following:

1.1, 1.3, 1.6, 2, 2.4, 3, 3.6, 4.3, 5.1, 6.2, 7.5, 9.1

The E24 range increases in increments of approximately 10%. The additional values of the E24 series are not often used.

Coded Letters

Practically all resistors use colour coding, but there are a few (mainly) close tolerance types which instead have the value marked using letters and numbers. The normal method uses four characters, and the first three indicate the value using what is basically the circuit diagram method. The only difference is that a value such as 560 ohms would be marked as "K56" (0.56k) rather than 560R (560 ohms). This is necessary because only three characters are available to show the value, and a value marking such as 560R clearly has one character too many. The final character is always a letter, and it indicates the tolerance using this method of coding.

Letter	Tolerance
F	1%
G	2%
H	2.5%
J	5%
K	10%
M	20%

These examples should help to clarify this system.

K10K	100 ohms 10%
1K0J	1k 5%
10KG	10k 2%
M10G	100k 2%
1M0F	1M 1%
10MK	10M 10%

9

5R6K	5.6 ohms 10%
56RJ	56 ohms 5%
K56J	560 ohms 5%
5K6G	5.6k 2%
56KF	56k 1%
M56F	560k 1%
5M6M	5.6M 20%

On a few resistors the value is marked in standard circuit diagram fashion, with a final digit again indicating the tolerance. This requires a fifth character for some values. A 220 ohm 2% resistor would then be marked "220RG", rather than "K22G".

Power Rating

Apart from its value and tolerance rating, a resistor also has a power rating. This is not marked on the component in any way, and if it is not known it can usually be gauged from the physical size of the component. The larger the resistor, the higher its power rating. For most modern circuits the power rating of the resistors is not of great importance because they consume so little power. Even using subminiature 0.125 watt resistors there is little chance of them burning out. In fact the opposite is more likely to be a problem, with there being too little space available if (say) a one watt resistor is used where a 0.25 watt type is called for.

High power rating resistors are occasionally used in circuits such as power amplifiers and power supplies. In the past modified versions of the resistor colour code were often used for high power resistors, but these codes are now obsolete. For modern high power resistors the value is either marked using the standard four band method, or the four or five character methods are used. For one or two watt components colour coding is the most common method, but for higher power types the value is almost invariably marked using the letters and numbers method.

Capacitors

Capacitors are used in large numbers in most electronic circuits, and are usually outnumbered only by the resistors.

Some types are similar in appearance to resistors, with a lead-out wire at each end of a tubular body, but they are generally much larger than normal 0.25 watt resistors. Capacitors of this type are "axial" capacitors, and this is a term which can be applied to any component which has a tubular body and a lead-out wire at each end.

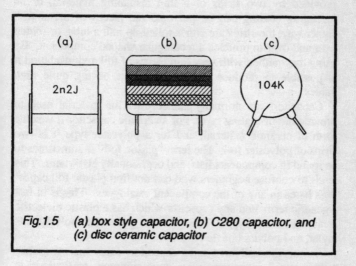

Fig. 1.5   (a) box style capacitor, (b) C280 capacitor, and (c) disc ceramic capacitor

Although at one time most capacitors were of the axial variety, or a sort of flattened version of it, the advent of printed circuit boards led to the development of different types. These printed circuit mounting ("PC") capacitors are designed for vertical mounting, and have the two leadout wires coming from the same end. Figure 1.5 shows three common forms of printed circuit mounting capacitor. These are the "box" style used for many plastic foil capacitors, the C280 polyester style, and the disc ceramic type. Ceramic capacitors are also available with rectangular bodies, and these are called ceramic plate capacitors. These days they are also available in the "box" style encapsulation.

Capacitors have names such as polyester, polystyrene, ceramic, etc., but what do these names mean? A capacitor is basically just two metal plates with a very thin layer of insulation in between. The insulating layer is known as the "dielectric" incidentally. In order to obtain reasonably high values it is necessary to have quite large plates, but physically huge capacitors are not a very practical proposition. In order to obtain high values in a physically small component the metal plates are in the form of strips of metal foil. The insulation is provided by two strips of a thin insulating material, or an insulating coating can be put onto the pieces of metal foil. Either way, the strips are either rolled-up into a tube, or folded over and over to produce a rectangular shaped component. By using this method with very thin pieces of foil and insulation it is possible to produce small components having quite high values.

Capacitors are normally named after the material used to provide the insulating layer. For a ceramic capacitor it is some form of ceramic material, and for a polyester type it is two strips of polyester foil. The term "plastic foil" is sometimes to be found in components lists, and occasionally elsewhere. This tends to confuse beginners who can not find plastic foil capacitors listed in any of the component catalogues. This is in fact a generic term, and any capacitor which has a plastic dielectric is a plastic foil type. This includes polyester, polystyrene, mylar, and polycarbonate types.

At one time silvered mica capacitors (also known as just "silver mica" capacitors) were quite common, particularly in radio receivers. This type of capacitor is still available, and where a very high quality low value capacitor is required it remains a good choice. The lack of popularity is probably due to the relatively high price of silvered mica capacitors. Also, they are relatively large considering their low values. Originally these capacitors were extremely large (often around 30 to 50 millimetres long), they had the sort of squashed axial shape shown in Figure 1.6(a). Modern silvered mica capacitors are usually much smaller than the originals, and have the printed circuit mounting encapsulation shown in Figure 1.6(b).

Polystyrene capacitors seem to have largely ousted silvered mica types these days. Unlike most other types of capacitors, polystyrene types are usually in the form of rather fat axial components. Like silvered mica capacitors, polystyrene types are only generally available in low to medium values, and are

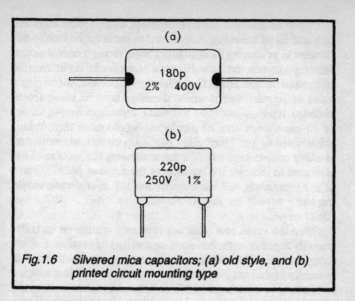

Fig. 1.6   Silvered mica capacitors; (a) old style, and (b)
printed circuit mounting type

relatively large for a given value. Consequently, they are not
readily interchangeable with other plastic foil types, and it is
best if they are only used where a polystyrene capacitor is mentioned specifically in the components list.

Values

The values of capacitors are expressed in farads, and this unit is
named after Faraday. The farad is an extremely large unit, and
practical capacitors generally have values that are only a
minute fraction of a farad. Consequently, most capacitors have
their values expressed in terms of microfarads, nanofarads, or
picofarads. A microfarad is one millionth of a farad. A nano-
farad is equal to one thousand picofarads, and one microfarad
is equal to one thousand nanofarads. This table shows the rela-
tionship between these three units of measurement.

	Microfarad	Nanofarad	Picofarad
Microfarad	1	1000	1000000
Nanofarad	0.001	1	1000
Picofarad	0.000001	0.001	1

The word micro is often abbreviated to the Greek letter mu (μ), and farad is usually abbreviated to the letter F. Due to difficulties in producing Greek letters using modern computerised drawing systems, etc., the letter "u" (always in lower case) is often used instead of the Greek letter mu. A capacitor having a value of 10 microfarads would therefore have its value abbreviated to 10μF, or just 10μ. Similarly, capacitors having values of 10 nanofarads and 10 picofarads would have their values abbreviated to just "10n" and "10p". On circuit diagrams, and in many components lists, the letter showing the units in use is also used to indicate the position of the decimal point. Values of 3.3 picofarads, 4.7 nanofarads, and 2.2 microfarads would therefore appear on circuit diagrams as "3p3", "4n7", and "2u2" respectively.

Often the value of a capacitor is simply written on its body, possibly together with the tolerance and (or) its maximum operating voltage. The tolerance rating may be omitted, and it is generally higher for capacitors than for resistors. Most modern resistors have tolerances of 5% or better, but for capacitors the tolerance rating is generally 10% or 20%. The tolerance figure is more likely to be marked on a close tolerance capacitor than a "bog standard" 10% or 20% type.

Probably the most popular form of value marking on modern capacitors is for the value to be written on the components in some slightly cryptic form. Small ceramic capacitors generally have the value marked in much the same way that the value is written on a circuit diagram. Values of 2.2 picofarads and 22 picofarads would therefore be written on the components as "2p2" and "22p" respectively. For values from 100p to 820p the markings can sometimes be a bit confusing. A value such as 470 picofarads might be marked as "470p", but on most small ceramic capacitors it would appear in the form "n47". In other words, 0.47 nanofarads, which is the same as 470 picofarads.

A similar system is commonly used on higher value plastic foil capacitors. For example, one of the capacitors in my spares box is marked "33nJ250". The value of this component is clearly 33 nanofarads. The "J" indicates its tolerance using the same method that is used for some resistors, and which was described previously. In this case a letter "J" indicates a tolerance rating of 5%. The "250" indicates that the maximum voltage rating of the component is 250 volts d.c. On the higher value capacitors the value marking can look a little strange at first due to the absence of the leading zero. For example, a value of 0.47 microfarads (470 nanofarads) will often be marked as "µ47" rather than "470n" or "0µ47".

On larger ceramic capacitors, plus some plastic foil types, the value is marked using three numbers. This method is similar to the resistor colour code, where the first three colours indicate the value. The first two numbers are the first two digits of the value. The third number is the multiplier, and indicates the number of zeros that must be added to produce the full value. The value is always in picofarads incidentally. As an example, a capacitor marked "473" would have a value of 47 nanofarads. The first two digits of the value are obviously "47", and three zeros must be added to this in order to give the value in picofarads. This gives a value of 47000 picofarads, which is the same as 47 nanofarads.

The three number value marking is often followed by a letter which indicates the component's tolerance. This method of tolerance marking is, once again, the same as the one for resistors that was described previously. For example, a letter "K" indicates a tolerance of 10%. There may be some other markings, such as the maximum voltage rating, but any additional markings are often just manufacturers logos, batch numbers, etc., and are of no practical importance.

Colour Code
Some years ago it was quite common for capacitors to be marked with colour codes, but relatively few capacitors are colour coded these days. At one time virtually all the C280 style plastic foil capacitors were colour coded, but this method of value marking is one that is only encountered infrequently at present. Figure 1.7 shows how the C280 method of coding operates. Once again, the method used is firmly based on the standard four band resistor coding. The first three bands indicate the value in normal resistor fashion, but the value is in picofarads. To convert this into a value in nanofarads it is merely necessary to divide by 1000. Divide the marked value by 1000000 if a value in microfarads is required.

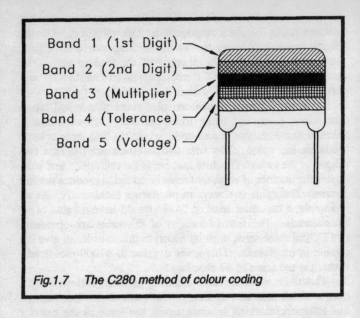

Fig.1.7   The C280 method of colour coding

The fourth band indicates the tolerance, but the colour coding used is different to the resistor equivalent. The fifth band shows the maximum working voltage of the component. Details of the fourth and fifth band colour coding is provided in this table.

Colour	Band 4	Band 5
Black	20%	–
White	10%	–
Green	5%	–
Orange	2.5%	–
Red	2%	250V
Brown	1%	–
Yellow	–	400V

Most of the C280 style capacitors you obtain are likely to be 250 volt types, but 400 volt types are sold by some retailers. Values of 220n or less generally have a tolerance of 20 percent, with higher values having a tolerance of 10 percent.   A component having the colour code orange – orange – yellow – white – red would have a value of 330n (330000p), a tolerance of 10 percent, and a maximum operating voltage of 250 volts.

Electrolytics

So far we have only considered non-polarised capacitors. Like resistors, these can be connected into circuit either way round. Polarised capacitors have positive (+) and negative (–) terminals, and must be connected into circuit the right way round.

By far the most common form of polarised capacitor is the electrolytic type. Apart from a few high-grade types, electrolytic capacitors are rather low in quality. The ideal capacitor has perfect insulation, and lets no leakage current pass through its dielectric. No "real world" capacitor has an infinite resistance through its dielectric, but for practically all non-polarised types the leakage resistance is so high as to be of no practical importance in most circuits. For electrolytic types, even when connected with the correct polarity, the leakage current is often quite significant. This precludes their use in critical applications. Another problem with electrolytic capacitors is that they mostly have quite high tolerances. A tolerance rating of +50% and –20% is quite normal, and some have tolerances as high as +100% and –50%!

Electrolytic capacitors may seem to be of little practical value, but they do have one all-important advantage. Non-polarised capacitors having values of more than about 2.2 microfarads are not generally available. Non-polarised capacitors of about one microfarad in value tend to be quite large, and relatively expensive. Electrolytic capacitors having values from about 0.47 microfarads to several thousand microfarads are readily available. Except where very high values and (or) high voltage ratings are required, electrolytic capacitors are quite small and reasonably inexpensive. Something like a 2200 microfarad 50 volt electrolytic is likely to be quite sizeable and relatively expensive, but large capacitors of this type are only used in power supplies and a few other applications. As yet, technology can not offer a better alternative to large electrolytic capacitors.

Although electrolytic capacitors have comparatively poor performance figures, they are still perfectly adequate for many applications. However, due to their inadequacies an electrolytic type should never be used where the circuit designer has specified a non-electrolytic capacitor.

With non-polarised capacitors the voltage rating is usually of little practical importance. Most capacitors have voltage ratings of around 100 to 400 volts, but most modern circuits operate on supply potentials of only about three to 30 volts. Where a high voltage rating is important, this fact should be emphasised in the components list and the text of the book or magazine article.

The situation is rather different with electrolytic capacitors, where higher value components with voltage ratings as low as 10 volts are quite commonplace. Components lists normally give a voltage rating for all electrolytic types. With the smaller electrolytics the voltage rating will probably be given as something like 50 or 63 volts. In the vast majority of cases the actual working voltage of the capacitor will be far less than this voltages rating. A voltage rating of 50 or 63 volts is quoted simply because these lower values are only generally available with voltage ratings of about 50 volts or more. It is still advisable to use components having at least the specified voltage rating.

With larger electrolytics the specified voltage ratings are likely to be only slightly higher than the actual working voltages. It is then essential to use components having voltage ratings at least as high as the figures specified in the components lists. Be warned that an electrolytic capacitor used beyond its voltage rating is quite likely to explode with a loud "crack". The same thing is likely to happen if an electrolytic capacitor is connected with the wrong polarity. Always be careful to double-check the polarity of electrolytics once you have completed a project. Pay special attention to any that are connected direct across the project's supply rails.

There are two normal physical forms for electrolytic capacitors, and these days the type for vertical mounting (Figure 1.8(a)) is probably the most common. These are known as "PC" (printed circuit) or radial electrolytics. The polarity is indicated by "+" and (or) "−" signs on the body of the component. It is now more or less standard for the negative leadout wire to be shorter than the positive one, making it possible to fit a capacitor of this type correctly without having to carefully look for a plus or minus sign.

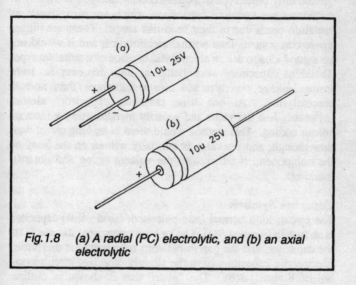

Fig.1.8   (a) A radial (PC) electrolytic, and (b) an axial electrolytic

The other normal type of electrolytic is the axial type, which has the usual tubular body and leadout wire at each end. The polarity of axial electrolytics is indicated by plus and minus signs on the body, but it is also shown by an indentation around one end of the body (Figure 1.8(b)). This indentation is near the positive leadout wire.

Some large electrolytic capacitors are known as "can" types, and these are rather like outsize radial electrolytics. However, instead of leadout wires they have tags to which leads can be soldered. In normal use they are mounted in metal clips on the base panel of the case or the chassis of the project, with the tag-end uppermost. Capacitors of this type are only available in values of a few thousand microfarads or more, and usually have fairly high voltage ratings (about 50 volts or more). Capacitors of this type are less common than they once were, because improvements in electrolytic technology have resulted in the physical size of electrolytics steadily reducing over recent years. This has reduced the need for large can-type electrolytic capacitors.

The only other type of polarised capacitor you are likely to encounter are tantalum capacitors, which are also known as tantalum beads due to their bead-like shape. These are higher grade components than normal electrolytics, and it would not be a good idea to use an electrolytic in place of a tantalum type. Tantalum capacitors work better at high frequencies, have lower leakage currents, and closer tolerances than normal electrolytics. At one time tantalum capacitors almost invariably had the value and polarity marked using a form of colour coding. This method would seem to be long out of date now though, and the value is normally written on the body of the component, together with the voltage rating and polarity markings.

Capacitor Symbols

The circuit for a normal (non-polarised, fixed value) capacitor is shown in Figure 1.9(a). The two bars represent the plates of the capacitor, and the gap in between represents the dielectric. Electrolytic capacitors have the slightly modified circuit symbol of Figure 1.9(b). The "plate" that is shown in outline denotes the positive terminal, but a plus sign is usually included as well. There are such things as reversible electrolytic capacitors which do not require a polarising voltage. These can be used like non-polarised capacitors, which is what they are. Reversible electrolytics are something of a rarity, and I have only used one of these in about 35 years in electronics. They have the circuit symbol of Figure 1.9(c). Tantalum capacitors have the normal capacitor circuit symbol with the addition of a plus sign to indicate the polarity (Figure 1.9(d)).

Diodes

These are the most simple components in the semiconductor family. They have the appearance shown in Figure 1.10(a), and the circuit symbol shown in Figure 1.10(b). The action of a diode is to act as a sort of electronic valve, permitting an electric current to flow in one direction but not the other. In terms

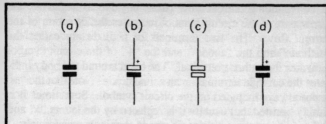

Fig.1.9   Capacitor circuit symbols (a) normal capacitor,
           (b) electrolytic, (c) reversible electrolytic, and
           (d) tantalum

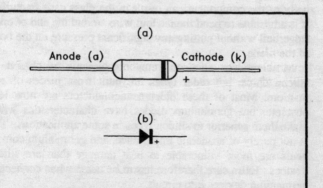

Fig.1.10   (a) Physical appearance of a diode, and (b)
           diode circuit symbol

of conventional current flow (from positive to negative), the arrow part of the circuit symbol indicates the direction of the current flow. The two terminals of a diode are called the "cathode" and the "anode", and the "+" of the circuit symbol indicates the cathode terminal. The band around the body indicates the cathode terminal on an actual diode. Note that the "+" is not always included on the circuit symbol. Sometimes it is simply omitted, but usually it is replaced by the letters "a" and "k" to indicate the anode and cathode terminals respectively.

Most electronic components are reasonably tough and do not need to be handled particularly carefully. There are a few exceptions though, and some of the box style capacitors can easily end up with a leadout wire detached if they are not handled with due respect. Diodes are also relatively fragile. The modern smaller types are rather tougher than older style types having glass encapsulations. In particular, germanium diodes such as the popular OA90 and OA91 types seem to be very vulnerable.

Obviously any component which has a glass case needs to be treated with due care to avoid shattering the case. With a diode it is advisable to proceed carefully when bending the leadout wires through right angles so that it can be fitted onto a circuit board. Holding the body of the component in one hand and then using the other hand to bend a leadout wire close to the body of the component can result in the glass case fracturing. It is advisable to bend the leadout wire around the end of one's fingernail without putting any significant pressure on the body of the diode.

Most modern semiconductor components are based on silicon chips, but older types are built from pieces of germanium. Most of these older semiconductors are now long obsolete, but germanium diodes have characteristics which make them superior to silicon types in some applications. This is not purely of academic importance, and germanium components are more vulnerable to heat damage than are silicon devices. Extra care therefore has to be taken when connecting germanium devices into circuit.

Diodes do not have values in the same way as resistors and capacitors. They do have principle ratings such as the maximum voltages and currents they can handle, but diodes are

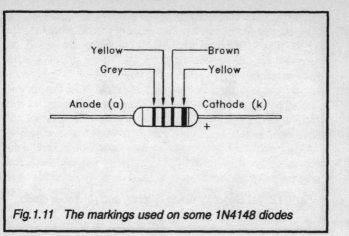

Fig.1.11 The markings used on some 1N4148 diodes

normally sold under type numbers rather than by current and voltage ratings.

These days some diodes have multiple bands which show the type number using a system that is similar to the resistor colour code. You are only likely to encounter this method of marking on some examples of the ever popular 1N4148 silicon diode. Each digit in the "4148" part of the type number is represented by a coloured band, and the coding used seems to be the same method that is used for the first two digits of a resistor colour code. Therefore, the bands around a 1N4148 diode are yellow – brown – yellow – grey (Figure 1.11). With several bands around a diode, how do you determine its polarity? The first band is the one nearest to the cathode (+) leadout wire, and this band should be substantially thicker than the others.

Zener Diodes

There are several special types of diode, but there are only two of these that you are likely to encounter. One of them is the Schottky diode, which is a sort of superior grade silicon diode. Schottky diodes are suitable for operation at very high speeds, and they provide a lower voltage drop than ordinary silicon diodes. If a Schottky diode is specified for a project, satisfactory results are unlikely to be obtained using an ordinary silicon

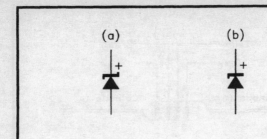

Fig.1.12 (a) Schottky diode symbol, and (b) zener diode symbol

type which has comparable voltage and current ratings. A Schottky diode has the modified diode symbol of Figure 1.12(a).

Although zener diodes were very popular at one time, they only seem to be used infrequently in modern circuits. They are used as the basis of voltage regulator circuits, but inexpensive integrated circuit voltage regulators have greatly reduced the need for zener diodes. They look much the same as ordinary diodes, and have the usual band to indicate the cathode (+) leadout wire. In components lists a zener diode can be specified by type number or simply as a zener diode having a particular operating voltage and power rating. Most components catalogues give both type numbers and principle parameters, so there should be no difficulty in locating a suitable component. Figure 1.12(b) shows the circuit symbol for a zener diode.

Rectifiers
One of the questions most frequently asked by beginners is "what is the difference between a diode and a rectifier?" The same basic action is provided by these two components, and in a sense they are different names for the same thing. However, the current convention is that a low power component is called a diode, and a higher power type is a rectifier. There is no "hard

24

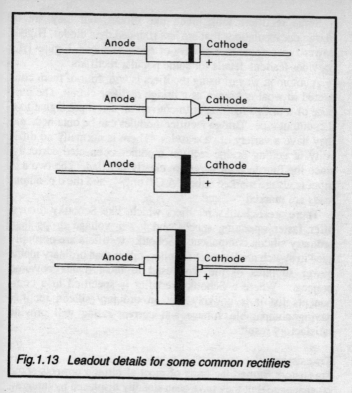

Fig.1.13 Leadout details for some common rectifiers

and fast" dividing line between the two, but a diode that is intended for use in power supply circuits would generally be regarded as a rectifier.

Diodes that are intended for non-power supply applications are generally accepted as diodes, even if their voltage and current ratings are only slightly lower than those of the smaller rectifiers. Strictly speaking though, they are all diodes, which is a term that also covers simple thermionic valves, or any component that provides an electronic valve action. In practice I suppose that the unofficial dividing line between diodes and rectifiers is at a current of one amp. Components that can handle a current of one amp or more tend to be regarded as rectifiers, while those with current ratings of less than one amp would generally be considered as diodes.

Some rectifiers look much like diodes, but they are in plastic encapsulations that are less rounded than diodes. Higher power types come in a variety of encapsulations. Figure 1.13 provides leadout details for some popular rectifiers.

A common way of using rectifiers is with four of them connected in what is known as a bridge rectifier circuit. The purpose of a bridge rectifier is to convert an a.c. input signal to a d.c. output type. Bridge rectifier modules can be obtained, and they have a variety of case styles. There is normally no difficulty in getting bridge rectifier modules connected correctly, since the four leadout wires are clearly labelled. The two a.c. input leads are marked either "A.C." or "~", and the d.c. output leads are marked "+" and "−".

There are Schottky rectifiers which, like Schottky diodes, offer faster operating speeds and lower voltage drops than ordinary silicon components. Schottky rectifiers are normally used in switch mode power supplies, rather than ordinary mains power supplies of the type used in most mains powered projects. Where a Schottky rectifier is specified in a components list it is unlikely that an ordinary silicon rectifier having comparable voltage and current rating will provide satisfactory results.

Transistors

Transistors formed the basis of most electronic projects about 20 years ago, but they have been steadily displaced by integrated circuits over the intervening years. Transistors are still to be found in many projects though, and you are likely to use a fair number of them. There are several types of transistor, but by far the most common type is the bipolar variety. These come in two basic types, which are n.p.n. and p.n.p. devices. The circuit symbols for these are shown in Figures 1.14(a) and 1.14(b) respectively.

These two types are very much the same as far as the user is concerned. The only significant difference between the two is that they require supplies of opposite polarities (n.p.n. circuits are normally negative earth whereas p.n.p. circuits are usually positive earth). Transistors have three terminals which are called the base, collector, and emitter. A few bipolar transistors do actually have a fourth leadout wire, but this just connects to

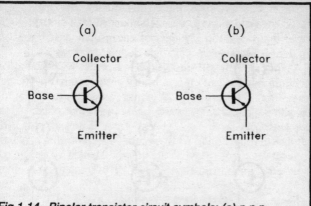

Fig.1.14 Bipolar transistor circuit symbols: (a) n.p.n., and (b) p.n.p.

the metal casing of the component. This lead is usually called the shield.

There are other types of transistor in common use, and these are the junction gate field effect transistor (Jfet or JUGFET), the metal oxide semiconductor field effect transistor (MOSFET), and the dual gate version of the MOSFET (DG MOSFET). These have the circuit symbols shown in Figures 1.15(a), 1.15(b), and 1.15(c) respectively. These are the symbols for N channel devices, which are comparable to n.p.n. bipolar transistors. Jfet and single gate MOSFETs are also available in P channel versions, which are the f.e.t. equivalent to p.n.p. bipolar transistors. These have the circuit symbols shown in Figures 1.15(d) and 1.15(e).

The three leadout wires of field effect transistors are the gate, drain, and source, which are roughly comparable to the base, collector, and emitter terminals (respectively) of bipolar types. Dual gate MOSFETs have two gate terminals, which are simply called gate 1 and gate 2.

At one time unijunction transistors were quite common, but they are now virtually obsolete. A transistor of this type can not provide amplification, and can not be used in most of the applications normally associated with transistors. Unijunctions are

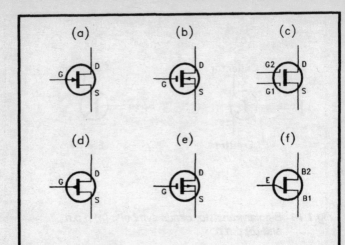

Fig.1.15   Further transistor symbols: (a) N channel Jfet,
(b) N channel MOSFET, (c) D.G. MOSFET,
(d) P channel Jfet, (e) P channel MOSFET, and
(f) unijunction

mainly used in oscillators, but there are now low cost integrated circuits which handle this task much more effectively. Hence they have fallen from favour and are not normally to be found in new designs. The circuit symbol for a unijunction transistor is shown in Figure 1.15(f).

Transistors are housed in a variety of metal and plastic encapsulations. Figures 1.16 and 1.17 provide leadout details for a number of popular transistors. As is the convention for transistor leadout diagrams, these show the components viewed looking onto their underside (i.e. with the leadout wires pointing towards you). In the case of plastic power transistors, they are viewed looking onto the metal pad on the underside.

Thyristor and Triacs

These devices are used in d.c. and a.c. control circuits respectively. The smaller types mostly have TO5 metal cases, and look much like medium power transistors such as the BFY51,

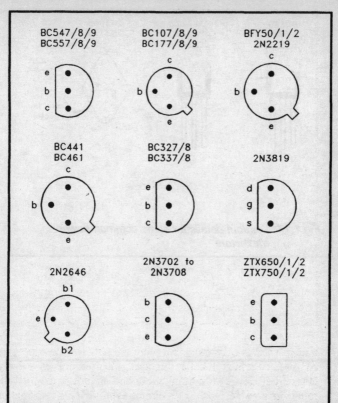

Fig.1.16 Leadout details for some popular transistors

etc. Like transistors, thyristors and triacs both have three lead-out wires. Thyristors are also known as silicon controlled rectifiers, or just s.c.r.s.

The three leadout wires of a thyristor are the anode, cathode, and gate. A thyristor has the circuit symbol shown in Fig.1.18(a). The terminals of a triac are called main terminal 1 (MT1), main terminal 2 (MT2), and gate. The MT1 and MT2 terminals are alternatively known as anode 1 (A1) and anode 2 (A2). Figure 1.18(b) shows the circuit symbol for a triac. Figure 1.19 shows leadout details for a few common thyristors

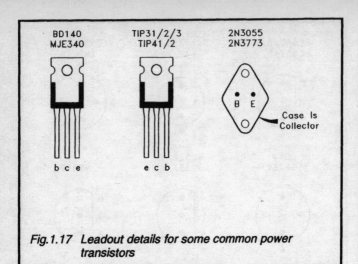

Fig.1.17 Leadout details for some common power transistors

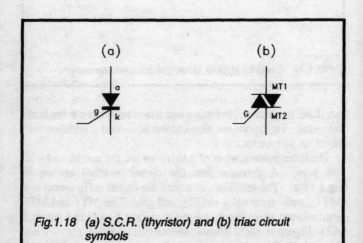

Fig.1.18 (a) S.C.R. (thyristor) and (b) triac circuit symbols

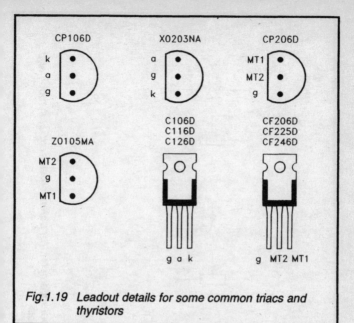

Fig.1.19 Leadout details for some common triacs and thyristors

and triacs. In common with transistor leadout diagrams, it is the convention for these to be base views.

Potentiometers

This is a form of variable resistor, and a normal rotary type has the general appearance shown in Figure 1.20(a). The circuit symbols for a potentiometer are shown in Figure 1.20(b). There are also slider potentiometers, but these do not seem to be used a great deal in modern designs for the home constructor. This is possibly due to their higher cost and awkward mounting requirements.

In components lists potentiometers are usually specified as being "log" (logarithmic) or "lin" (linear). Most applications require linear potentiometers, and volume controls are the only common application for logarithmic types. A project will actually work if you use a potentiometer of the wrong type, but the result will be a rather awkward control characteristic. For

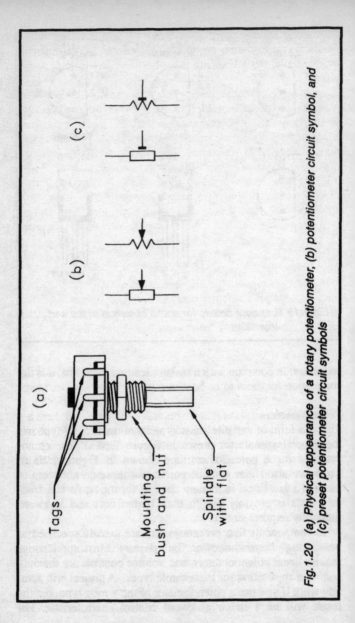

Fig. 1.20 (a) Physical appearance of a rotary potentiometer, (b) potentiometer circuit symbol, and (c) preset potentiometer circuit symbols

Tags

Mounting bush and nut

Spindle with flat

(a)

(b)

(c)

example, if a linear potentiometer is used as a volume control, advancing it from zero produces a very large increase in volume initially, but advancing it further then has little apparent affect.

Most projects require carbon potentiometers, but wirewound types are occasionally needed where relatively high powers are involved. A carbon potentiometer has a track that is made from a thin deposit of carbon, whereas a wirewound type has a track that is made from resistance wire wound around a ring-like plastic or ceramic former. Apart from being able to handle higher powers, wirewound potentiometers also provide greater precision than carbon types, which can be beneficial in some applications. They are usually somewhat larger than carbon types, and are only generally available in linear versions. Carbon potentiometers are available in values from about 1k to around 2M2, and wirewound types are available with values from a few ohms to about 100k.

As well as logarithmic and linear potentiometers, there is a third type called antilogarithmic (antilog) or reverse logarithmic. These are only used in a few specialised applications, such as some audio signal generators, and are little used by amateurs. There is another type of potentiometer – the dual gang type. A dual gang potentiometer is basically just two potentiometers combined into a single component, and having a common control shaft. Potentiometers of this type are mainly used in the tone and volume controls of stereo equipment.

Potentiometers are available in preset versions, and these are to be found in many electronic projects. Figure 1.20(c) shows the circuit symbols for preset potentiometers. They are not controls of the type that are mounted on the front panels of equipment, and they are not normally operated via a control knob at all. They are mounted on the circuit board and are adjusted using a tool (which is normally just a small screwdriver). They are used in critical parts of a circuit where it is necessary to accurately set certain operating conditions in order to obtain satisfactory results. Once adjusted correctly, the preset resistor or resistors may never need to be adjusted again.

Preset resistors are available in a variety of shapes and sizes. Some are fully cased, while others have open construction. The open type are sometimes called "skeleton" presets. Preset resistors are made in both logarithmic and linear versions, but only the linear type are readily available to amateur users. Components lists do not normally specify whether presets are logarithmic or linear types, but unless stated otherwise they can be assumed to be ordinary linear presets. There are vertical and horizontal mounting presets, which are respectively adjusted from the side and from above. Apart from any other considerations, their mounting arrangements are very different, and they are not physically interchangeable. There are very high quality presets known as multi-turn "trimpots", which are used where very accurate adjustment and good long term stability are needed.

Variable Capacitors

Capacitors having variable values are available, but only in a rather limited range of values. Small types have maximum values of around five to 10 picofarads, and large types have maximum values that are still only about 500 picofarads. Variable capacitors are mainly used in radio applications, such as the tuning controls of radio receivers. They vary considerably in physical appearance, but they all consist basically of two sets of metal plates. One set of plates is fixed, and the other can be rotated via the control shaft. By rotating the shaft the two sets of plates can be made to mesh together by any required degree, but they do not come into physical or electrical contact with each other. The more the plates are meshed together, the higher the capacitance value produced.

The plates of high quality variable capacitors are normally separated by air, and appropriately these are known as air-spaced capacitors. Variable capacitors of this type have to be built to a high degree of precision, and are relatively expensive. They are also comparatively easy to damage, but otherwise seem to have very long operating lives. Many air-spaced variable capacitors are of open construction, and they must therefore be handled carefully if damage to the plates is to be avoided. Bent plates can usually be pressed back into place without too much difficulty, but prevention is better than cure. Avoid getting small pieces of excess solder or swarf into air spaced variable capacitors.

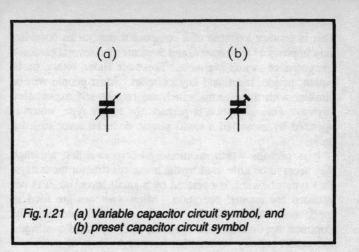

Fig. 1.21 (a) Variable capacitor circuit symbol, and
(b) preset capacitor circuit symbol

The alternative to air-spaced variable capacitors is the solid dielectric variety. These are not radically different to the air spaced type, but the plates are usually much thinner and something less than rigid. Small sheets of plastic are used to separate the two sets of plates and provide electrical isolation between then. Solid dielectric variable capacitors are generally much smaller than air-spaced equivalents, and significantly less expensive. However, they are usually unsuitable for use at high frequencies, such as in short wave receivers. Do not use a solid dielectric type if a components list specifies an air-spaced capacitor.

There are preset variable capacitors, which are also known as "trimmers" or "trimmer capacitors". These are available in a variety of shapes and sizes, in both air-spaced and solid dielectric varieties. Like preset resistors, they are adjusted using a tool, which is normally a small screwdriver. However, in some case the metal blade of a screwdriver would affect the component's capacitance, making it necessary to use a plastic trimming tool instead. The circuit symbols for variable and trimmer capacitors are shown in Figure 1.21(a) and 1.21(b) respectively.

Switches

This is another example of a component that varies considerably in physical appearance, and there are also several common categories of switch available. These are slider, rotary, pushbutton, toggle, lever, and key switches. Most people will be familiar with these terms which are largely self explanatory anyway. One exception is perhaps the toggle type, which is operated by means of a small plastic or metal lever called a dolly.

It is perhaps worth mentioning micro-switches, although they seem to be little used by the home constructor these days. This type of switch is operated by a small lever, but it is not intended for manual operation. Micro-switches are used in applications where switches must be operated automatically. Common applications are robotics, coin operated machines, and model railway layouts that have some form of automatic control.

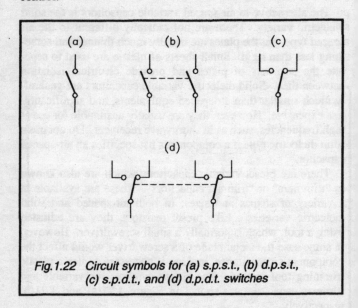

Fig.1.22 Circuit symbols for (a) s.p.s.t., (b) d.p.s.t., (c) s.p.d.t., and (d) d.p.d.t. switches

Electrically the most simple form of switch is the single pole single throw (s.p.s.t.) type, and the circuit symbol for this kind

36

of switch is shown in Figure 1.22(a). This is just a simple on/off switch which is shown in the off position in the diagram (as is the convention for a normal s.p.s.t. switch). Where two s.p.s.t. switches are contained in a single mechanism so that they operate in unison, they form a double pole single throw (d.p.s.t.) switch. This type of switch has the circuit symbol shown in Figure 1.22(b).

A double throw switch is one which has three tags. The "pole" tag connects to one or other of the other two tags, depending on the setting of the switch. This type of switch is also known (for obvious reasons) as a changeover switch. Figure 1.22(c) shows the circuit symbol for a single pole double pole (s.p.d.t.) switch. Figure 1.22(d) shows the circuit symbol for a double pole version (a d.p.d.t. switch).

On/off switches are sometimes combined with potentiometers, usually to provide a combined on/off switch and volume control. The switch is normally a d.p.s.t. type, and in a mains powered project both sides of the mains supply can therefore be switched. For battery powered projects it is generally deemed acceptable to switch only one supply rail, and one pole of the switch can then be left unused.

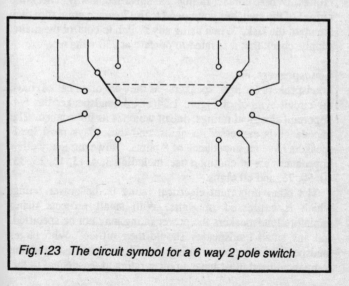

Fig.1.23 The circuit symbol for a 6 way 2 pole switch

Switches having these four contact arrangements can be obtained in any of the six types of construction mentioned previously. More complicated switches are generally only available in rotary form, although some three and four pole types are available as toggle switches, etc. The more complex rotary switches are sometimes referred to as "wafer" switches. Rotary switches are normally specified as having "x" number of ways and "y" number of poles. Thus, the switch represented by the circuit symbol of Figure 1.23 would be described as a 6 way 2 pole switch.

Many of the rotary switches currently available have an adjustable end-stop so that they can be used in applications where the full number of ways are not required. For instance, many 6 pole 2 way rotary switches can be used for 2, 3, 4, 5, or 6 way operation by giving the end-stop the appropriate setting.

In addition to the number of ways and poles, switches have contact ratings. These are the maximum voltage and current that a given switch can handle. In many components lists the current and voltage ratings are not mentioned, and this is simply due to the fact that only low voltages and currents are involved. Consequently, any normal switch has adequate ratings. Where contact ratings are specified, always check the ratings of the switches you intend to use to make quite sure they are up to the task. When using any switch to control the mains supply, check that it is rated to operate at 230 volts a.c.

Loudspeakers, etc.
Loudspeakers (or just "speakers" as they are often called) have the circuit symbol of Figure 1.24(a). A loudspeaker has two important electrical ratings, one of which is its impedance. The impedance is expressed in ohms, and these days most loudspeakers have an impedance of 8 ohms. However, many other impedances are in common use, including 3, 4, 15, 16, 25, 35, 40, 50, 75, and 80 ohms.

The other important electrical rating is the power rating, which is expressed in watts. With small projects using miniature loudspeakers the power rating may not be specified, and any small loudspeaker should then suffice. With larger loudspeakers the power rating should be specified, and the component used must have a power rating at least equal to the specified rating. Component catalogues specify the physical sizes of loudspeakers. For round types this is simply the overall diameter, and for elliptical units it is the overall length and breadth.

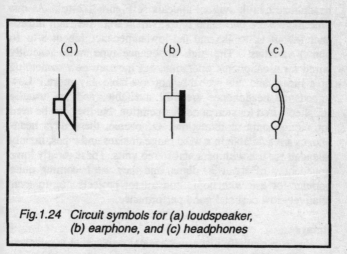

Fig.1.24   Circuit symbols for (a) loudspeaker,
(b) earphone, and (c) headphones

It is important to handle loudspeakers with due care, since they have a diaphragm that is made from a fairly flimsy material. Traditionally the diaphragm is made from paper based material, but plastics and even metals are used for some modern loudspeakers. Whatever the material used, it is all too easy to accidentally knock a hole in it. The coil and some other parts of a loudspeaker are also quite vulnerable to physical damage. Avoid dropping small pieces of wire, etc., into the interior of a loudspeaker.

Most people will be familiar with earpieces, since they are often supplied with transistor radios and portable cassette recorders. Two main types are available, which are the low impedance (8 ohm) dynamic type, and the high impedance (about 100 to 200k) crystal type. These both have the circuit symbol which appears in Figure 1.24(b). It is worth noting that although these two types of earphone may be similar in appearance, they have completely different electrical characteristics, and in most cases a project will only work well with one

39

type or the other. A project designed for use with a crystal earphone is unlikely to work at all with a low impedance dynamic type.

Headphones should also be familiar to most people. The headphone circuit symbol appears in Figure 1.24(c). At one time there were two main types, which were the high impedance (about 1k to 4k) and the low impedance (about 8 to 16 ohms) varieties. The high impedance type were generally wired for monophonic operation, but they are now something of a rarity, and are probably not available any more. Low impedance headphones are still available, and are usually supplied wired for stereophonic operation (but they can be used for monophonic reproduction). Of course, these days headphones are available in a wide range of sizes and types, mainly intended for use with personal stereo units. These mostly have impedances of about 30 ohms, and they are becoming quite popular for use with home constructor projects due to their relatively low cost and good performance.

Relays
A relay is essentially just a mechanical switch that is operated via a solenoid (an electromagnet). Relays have several important parameters. The two important ratings for the coil are its nominal operating voltage and its resistance in ohms. It is important to use a relay which has the operating voltage specified in the components list. The coil resistance should be equal to or higher than the specified resistance.

The switch contacts have maximum voltage and current ratings. The d.c. and a.c. current ratings are usually different, with the d.c. rating being much lower. Therefore, if you are using the relay contacts to control a d.c. load, make sure you refer to the d.c. contact ratings. You must use a component that has contact current and voltage ratings at least equal to those specified by the circuit designer.

These days relays are usually mounted direct onto the printed circuit board, rather than being mounted off-board on the chassis or on some form of mounting bracket. It is then advisable to use the exact relay specified by the circuit designer. Other relays may have perfectly suitable electrical characteristics, but they are unlikely to fit onto the circuit board properly.

40

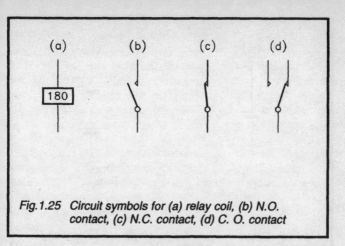

*Fig.1.25 Circuit symbols for (a) relay coil, (b) N.O.
contact, (c) N.C. contact, (d) C. O. contact*

Figure 1.25(a) shows the circuit symbol for a relay coil. The number within the box shows the coil resistance in ohms. The relay coils in a circuit are designated RLA, RLB, etc., and not RL1, RL2, etc. as one might have expected. The number beneath the marking shows the number of contacts associated with that particular relay coil. The relay contacts are annotated RLA1, RLA2, etc. for the first relay, RLB1, RLB2, etc., for any subsequent relay, and so on. Figures 1.25(b) to 1.24(d) respectively show the circuit symbols for normally open (N.O.) contacts, normally closed (N.C.) contacts, and a set of changeover (C.O.) contacts.

Batteries
This is another example of a component which should be familiar to all readers. A single cell has the circuit symbol of Figure 1.26(a), and a multi-cell type has the circuit symbol of Figure 1.26(b). The latter should always have the nominal battery voltage marked next to the symbol.

Lamps
A signal lamp has the circuit schematic of Figure 1.27(a), while an illuminating lamp has the one shown in Figure 1.27(b). These days filament bulbs are little used in electronic devices, with light emitting diodes (l.e.d.s) having almost totally

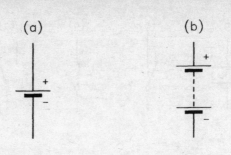

Fig.1.26 Circuit symbols for (a) single cell battery and (b) multi-cell battery

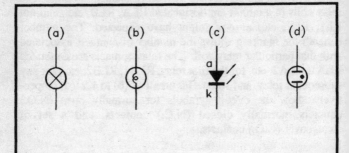

Fig.1.27 Circuit symbols for (a) signal lamp, (b) illuminating lamp, (c) L.E.D., and (d) neon

usurped them. A l.e.d. has the circuit symbol of Figure 1.27(c). One advantage of l.e.d.s is that they only need very low operating powers in order to produce high enough light levels for use as indicator lights. Another advantage is that they have extremely long operating lives, and with continuous or intermittent use should last for very many years.

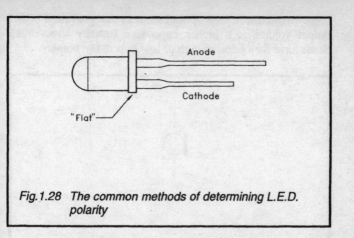

*Fig.1.28 The common methods of determining L.E.D.
polarity*

It is important to realise that a l.e.d. is a true diode, and that
it will only operate properly if it is connected the right way
round. The polarity of most l.e.d.s is indicated by having the
cathode (+) leadout wire slightly shorter than the anode leadout
wire. Also, the case is often flattened slightly on the cathode
side (Figure 1.28). If in doubt, the retailer's catalogue should
provide connection details. It is now possible to obtain l.e.d.s
in a variety of shapes and sizes, and for the more exotic types
it is advisable to check connection details in the retailer's
catalogue.

Neons are perhaps used rather less than was once the case,
but they are still popular as mains on/off indicators. They have
the circuit symbol shown in Figure 1.27(d). Neons intended for
use as mains indicators normally have built-in series resistors to
prevent an excessive current flow. Most neons which do not
have this resistor are not suitable for direct use on the mains
supply.

Microphones
These have the circuit symbol shown in Figure 1.29. Like ear-
phones, they are available in both crystal and magnetic (dynamic) types. There are also other types, but the electret variety is
the only other common form of microphone. Dynamic microphones have low impedances of about 200 ohms to 1k, but

some have built-in step-up transformers that provide a higher output voltage at a higher impedance (usually about 50k). Some have the option of high or low impedance outputs.

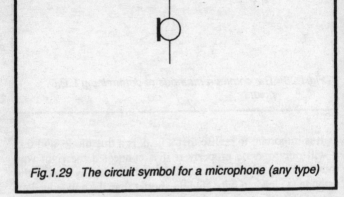

Fig.1.29   The circuit symbol for a microphone (any type)

Electret microphones normally require a small battery to power an integral preamplifier. This gives a low output impedance, but some electret types have a built-in step-up transformer that provides a high output impedance (again about 50k). Crystal microphones have a relatively high output level, but they effectively have a very high output impedance (about one or two megohms). Crystal microphones were once very popular, but now seem to be something of a rarity.

Coils, etc.
An inductor is a very simple component that is basically just a coil of wire. Inductors are often just referred to as coils, and they are also known as chokes. The basic circuit symbol for a coil is shown in Figure 1.30(a). The slightly modified circuit symbol of Figure 1.30(b) is used for a coil that has a ferrite or dust iron core. If the coil has a tapping (a connection made at other than one end of the winding or the other), this is indicated in the manner shown in Figure 1.30(c).

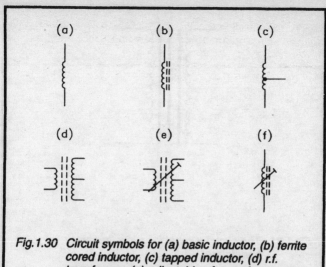

Fig.1.30   Circuit symbols for (a) basic inductor, (b) ferrite
cored inductor, (c) tapped inductor, (d) r.f.
transformer, (e) adjustable r.f. transformer, and
(f) adjustable inductor

Coils often have more than one winding, and they are then
called transformers. Transformers for use in radio frequency
(r.f.) and intermediate frequency (i.f.) stages have the circuit
schematic of Figure 1.30(d). Transformers for use at these higher frequencies often have adjustable cores, and they then have
the circuit symbol of Figure 1.30(e). An inductor can also have
an adjustable core, although this seems to be relatively rare.
Figure 1.30(f) shows the circuit symbol for an adjustable inductor. Transformers for use in low frequency applications such as
audio frequency amplifiers and mains power supplies have the
circuit symbol of Figure 1.31.

Photocells
At one time photoresistors were the most commonly used type
of photocell, but semiconductor photocells are now the more
popular form.   Photoresistors such as the ORP12 cadmium
sulphide cell are still quite popular though. The circuit symbols
for a photoresistor are shown in Figure 1.32(a).

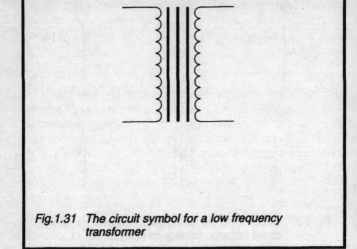

Fig.1.31 The circuit symbol for a low frequency transformer

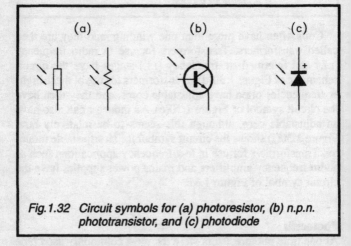

Fig.1.32 Circuit symbols for (a) photoresistor, (b) n.p.n. phototransistor, and (c) photodiode

Probably the most common form of semiconductor photo-cell is the phototransistor. This has the circuit symbol of Figure 1.32(b). Photodiodes are also quite common, and these have the circuit symbol shown in Figure 1.32(c). You may also encounter

46

devices called photo-darlington transistors. A device of this type is basically just a phototransistor driving an ordinary transistor, with the two components contained within the same case. This gives what is effectively a highly sensitive photo-transistor.

Meters

Although meters have to some extent been replaced by digital electronics plus l.e.d. and liquid crystal displays, they are still used to a significant extent in projects for the home constructor. There are two basic types of meter, which are the moving coil and moving iron varieties. Moving iron meters are little used in electronic projects as they have relatively low sensitivities, and non-linear scales. By contrast, moving coil meters have linear scales and can be designed to operate from very low currents. Moving coil meters are the only type you are likely to use in projects.

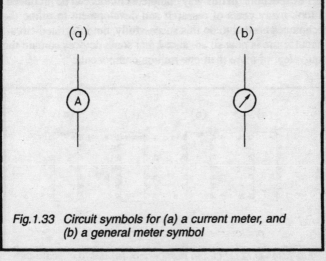

*Fig.1.33   Circuit symbols for (a) a current meter, and
(b) a general meter symbol*

Figure 1.33 shows two versions of the meter symbol. Sometimes the centre of the symbol is marked with the sensitivity of the meter, but these days the sensitivity is normally shown separately, beneath the component number.

47

The sensitivity of a meter can be so many volts, but virtually all the meters used in electronic projects are current rather than voltage meters. The main unit of current measurement is the ampere (or "amp"), but this is quite a large unit. Meters generally have full scale values specified in microamps (μA) or milliamps (mA). A milliamp is one thousandth of an amp, and a microamp is one thousandth of a milliamp (one millionth of an amp).

Integrated Circuits
It is now integrated circuits rather than discrete transistors that form the basis of most electronic projects. The normal method of manufacturing transistors is to produce thousands of them on a thin wafer of silicon, and to then cut up the slice into individual transistors. The basic idea with an integrated circuit is to manufacture the transistors in much the same way, but to then further process the silicon wafer to produce interconnections, plus other components such as diodes, resistors, and very low value capacitors. In this way complete circuits can be produced. It took many years of research and development to refine the techniques needed to do this successfully, but integrated circuit manufacture is now so advanced that some devices contain the equivalent of more than one million components.

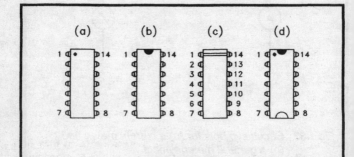

Fig.1.34   D.I.L.   I.C. pin numbering, (a) dot to indicate pin
1, (b) notch to indicate pins 1 and 14, (c) line to
indicate pins 1 and 14, (d) notch and dot plus a
confusing moulding mark

Physically, integrated circuits come in a wide variety of case styles. However, apart from some specialised types such as power devices and sensors, practically all the integrated circuits used by electronics hobbyists have plastic d.i.l. (dual in-line) encapsulations. These have various numbers of pins from six to 40, but the eight, 14, and 16 pin types are the most common.

Figure 1.34 shows the method of pin numbering used for d.i.l. integrated circuits. The example devices have 14 pins, but the method of pin numbering is the same for all d.i.l. integrated circuits. When viewed from above (i.e. with the pins pointing away from you) the pins are numbered in a counter-clockwise direction from pin one. Note that integrated circuit pinout diagrams are normally top views, which is the opposite to the convention for transistor leadout diagrams.

Sometimes pin one is indicated by a small dot or indentation in the plastic case. With other devices the pin-one end of the case is indicated by a line across the case, or by a notch in the case. Sometimes more than one method is implemented. It is always a good idea to look at integrated circuits carefully before deciding which is the pin-one end of the case. Many d.i.l. integrated circuits have moulding marks at the opposite end of the case which can look rather like the notch at a quick glance. Fitting an integrated circuit around the wrong way could quite easily result in it being ruined.

In a few cases special circuit symbols are used for integrated circuits (Figure 1.35). These are for operational amplifiers and the more simple logic functions. It is important to realise that a single integrated circuit can contain several operational amplifiers, NOR gates, or whatever. If IC4 in a circuit is a quad operational amplifier, it will be represented by four of the triangular operational amplifier symbols, and these will be marked IC4a, IC4b, IC4c, and IC4d. The vast majority of integrated circuits are simply represented by a rectangle, or in the case of a device which has several distinct sections, it may be represented by two or more rectangles. Again, the sections will be marked something like IC1a, IC1b, IC1c, etc. Every lead that emanates from an integrated circuit symbol should be marked with the appropriate pin number.

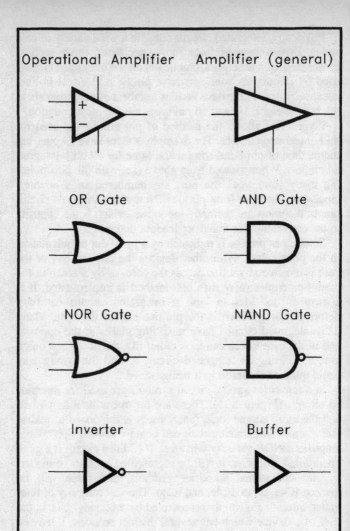

Fig.1.35 Common integrated circuit symbols (inputs on left, outputs on right of each symbol)

50

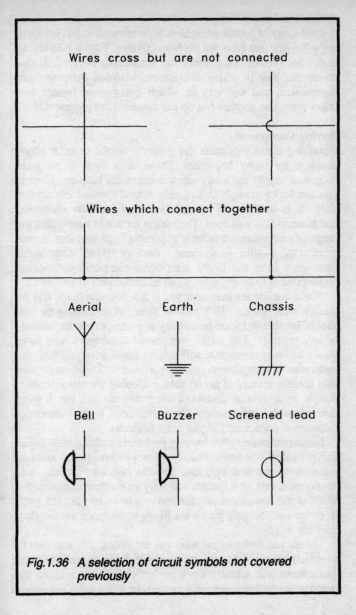

Fig.1.36 A selection of circuit symbols not covered previously

Other Symbols

A wide range of components have been covered so far, but there are still a few that have not yet been covered. Figure 1.36 shows the circuit symbols for components not already covered. It also shows the way in which connections between two wires are represented, and the way in which cross-overs (where two wires cross one another but do not connect) are represented.

Buying Components

Obtaining the components for projects seems to be a major problem for many beginners. These days there is no local source of supply for many electronic project builders. Even if you are lucky enough to live near a well stocked electronics shop, it is unlikely to be able to supply all the electronic components you will need. The reason for this is simply that the range of components available at present is so vast that no one store can handle everything. Two or three component catalogues from the larger mail order electronic component retailers have to be regarded as an essential part of the hobby.

These catalogues may cost you a few pounds, but it will be money well spent. With two or three large catalogues you should be able to locate practically any component for virtually any project. The larger component catalogues also have plenty of illustrations that will help to familiarise you with the vast range of components currently available. These catalogues also contain masses of useful data, including transistor leadout details, basic data on dozens of integrated circuits, etc. A great deal of useful information can be gleaned from component catalogues, particularly if you are a beginner.

Some companies offer bargain packs of surplus components, and provided you know exactly what you are doing, most of these packs are true bargains. For the beginner though, it is advisable to buy new, tested, and fully guaranteed components. Without the equipment and the know-how to sort out the good from the bad, bargain packs are likely to be more trouble than they are worth.

Unless you really know what you are doing, it is also best to avoid using substitute and near equivalent components. In most cases these will actually work perfectly well, but without the requisite experience you will be unable to spot the occasions where a substitute or near equivalent is not quite up to the task. If there are temporary supply difficulties it might be worthwhile trying the nearest component you can obtain or have in the spares box (such as using a 470k resistor instead of a 560k type). In general though, it is best to avoid this type of thing and only use the correct components.

Chapter 2

TOOLS FOR THE JOB

Obtaining and identify the components for a project is half the problem solved, leaving the minor matter of getting everything assembled correctly! Even a very simple project will require the use of some tools. Many of the tools used for electronic project construction are the type of thing that are already present in the average tool drawer. A hacksaw or junior hacksaw for example, is an everyday tool that is needed a great deal during project construction. However, there are some tools that are an essential part of the hobby, but are not to be found in the average toolkit.

Fortunately, a few reasonably inexpensive tools are all that you need to get started. As you progress to more complex projects you will probably have to add to you collection of tools. Initially though, it is probably best to start with a fairly modest toolkit, and gradually add to it as and when necessary. Otherwise there is a risk of buying expensive tools that will be rarely (if ever) used. In this chapter we will consider a wide range of tools, and their relative importance. We start with the all-important subject of soldering.

While the Iron's Hot

A soldering iron is an essential "tool of the trade", and is something that will probably not be present in your existing set of tools. Soldering irons for electronic work vary greatly in terms of price and sophistication. For project building there seems to be no real advantage in using an expensive up-market iron having accurate temperature stabilisation. A basic but good quality electric iron is perfectly adequate, and should only cost around £10-00. Most of the larger component catalogues list a few of the "Antex" soldering irons, and these offer good value for money. I have used these for over 30 years without any major problems.

Some very cheap soldering irons are available, but you need to be a little wary of these. The budget irons I have tried all seemed to produce too little heat. This restricts the rate at which soldered joints can be completed, if you can get the solder to melt at all!

Modern project construction is largely about large numbers of very small soldered connections, and this requires a small soldering iron. One having a rating of about 15 to 20 watts is suitable. It can be useful to have a more powerful soldering iron for the occasional larger joints, but an iron having a rating of about 17 watts should be just about sufficient to handle all your soldering requirements.

The "bit" of the iron is the part that is actually applied to the joint, and various shapes and sizes are available. Most small irons seem to be supplies with a bit of about 2.3 to 2.5 millimetres in diameter. This is suitable for most project construction. A smaller diameter is often better when soldering components onto intricate circuit boards, but the only smaller size available might be one of just one millimetre in diameter. This is slightly too small for general use. Unless finances stretch to two soldering irons, you have to use whichever size you find to be the best compromise. This is likely to be the bit of about 2.3 millimetres in diameter supplied with the iron.

Although soldering irons normally last many years, even if they receive a great deal of use, bits gradually wear and corrode away, and need occasional replacement. Fortunately, replacement bits are quite cheap, and mostly cost under £2-00.

Last Stand

A soldering iron stand should be regarded as an essential piece of equipment. A matching stand for a small soldering iron should only cost a few pounds, or you may be able to obtain the iron, stand, and some solder in a kit at an attractive price. The stand should last for many years, and it is likely to be the first and last stand that you will ever buy.

Apart from providing a safe resting place for the iron when it is hot, most stands also act as heatsinks. In other words, the stand helps to extract excess heat from the iron and radiate it into the surrounding air. The iron is designed to be able to produce soldered joints almost continuously, and this inevitably results in a certain amount of excess heat when it is not in use. Without the stand to remove this heat, the iron will get too hot, reducing the life of both the bit and the heating element.

Most soldering iron stands are equipped with one or two sponges. In use these are kept wet, and they are used to wipe the bit clean. The bit inevitably becomes contaminated with heavily oxidized solder, and the residue from flux. It is essential to clean this away periodically as it is impossible to produce good quality joints if the bit is too heavily coated.

Soldering On

There are many types of solder available, but for normal electronic work it is only a 60% tin – 40% lead type having a multiple flux core that should be used. This is generally available in two thicknesses, which are 18 s.w.g. (1.22 millimetres in diameter) and 22 s.w.g. (0.71 millimetres in diameter). In days gone-by it was the 18 s.w.g. size that was of most use, but most project construction consisted of soldering wires to large tags. Modern project construction is not completely devoid of this sort of thing, but most projects only require a few larger joints of this type. When soldering the components to circuit boards it is the thinner gauge that is easier to use.

If you are only going to obtain one type, then it is best to purchase 22 s.w.g. solder. This is usable for larger soldered joints, and is reasonably easy to use. The 18 s.w.g. variety is usable for intricate work on circuit boards, but is often quite awkward to use. There is a tendency to use too much solder, which gives problems with solder bridges and splashes producing short circuits. My advice would be to buy a fairly large reel of 22 s.w.g. solder, and a small amount of the 18 s.w.g. variety. A large reel of 22 s.w.g. solder will be relatively expensive to buy initially, but in the long term it is much cheaper than buying lots of small amounts. Also, it avoids the frustration of forever running out of solder when a project is 99% complete.

State of Flux

The purpose of the cores of flux is to remove any oxide or other coatings from the items that are being joined. It also helps the solder to flow nicely over each joint, producing a good electrical connection and a mechanically strong joint. There is a limit to the amount of surface contamination that the flux can deal with. If you apply the hot iron and solder to a badly contaminated lead you will probably find that the solder will not flow onto the lead.

This is much less of a problem than it was twenty or more years ago. Modern solders are more efficient at dealing with dirt, grease, etc., and components designed for modern production methods have leads and pins that do not corrode easily. You may occasionally encounter a lead that will not take the solder properly, and it is then necessary to scrape the lead with the small blade of a penknife in order to remove the contamination, and reveal bright, clean metal. The solder should then flow over the lead properly, producing a good strong joint.

Covering leads, tags, etc., with solder is a process known as tinning. When point-to-point wiring is being used (i.e. leads and tags are soldered directly to one another) it is advisable to tin all the tags and the ends of the leadout wires before attempting to complete any joints. Tinning is less important when fitting the components onto any form of printed circuit board. In fact there is normally no point in tinning the leads or the copper pads on the boards. The solder should flow over the joint properly without using any preparation. The only exception is where a lead or copper pad is obviously contaminated with a large amount of dirt or corrosion. It would then be prudent to clean away the contamination rather than proceeding in the hope that it will not produce any problems.

Joint Like This

As already pointed out, completing soldered joints on a printed circuit board is a rather different process to producing joints when carrying out point-to-point wiring. We will first consider the point-to-point method, which is probably the more difficult of the two.

When the soldering iron is first plugged in it will almost certainly produce a small amount of smoke. Do not worry about this, as it is quite normal, and is merely protective coatings on the bit and element burning away. As soon as the bit starts to get up to temperature, tin the tip with a small amount of solder. If you fail to do this quickly enough it is possible that the end of the bit will oxidize, making it impossible to tin it. This in turn makes it impossible to complete soldered joints until the bit has been cleaned and tinned. Once the bit has oxidized, getting it cleaned and properly tinned can be very problematic. In use the bit must be kept tinned with reasonably fresh solder, as this helps to make a good thermal connection between the bit and the soldered joint. This in turn helps the solder to flow properly over each joint.

As mentioned previously, the first step in making a connection is to tin the ends of the leads and the tags. In order to do this simply place the solder above the end of the lead or tag, apply the bit to the lead or tag, and then feed in a small amount of solder. If oxidation or other contamination prevents the solder from flowing properly, this will be immediately apparent. The solder will either collect on the bit or will fall onto the worktop. The lead or tag will become covered with flux, etc., rather than having a shiny coating of solder. If this happens, clean the lead or tag using a penknife and try again.

When the two surfaces to be joined have both been tinned, they are placed together and the bit and solder are applied to them using much the same method that was utilized for the tinning process. Provided an adequate quantity of solder is used, a good soldered joint should be produced.

It is worth making the point that with all electrical soldering the bit should be applied to the joint first, and then the solder should be fed in. Most beginners tend to place some solder onto the end of the bit, and then try to pour the solder onto the joint. This virtually guarantees a poor quality joint, if a joint can be produced at all. One problem is that much of the flux will burn away before the solder is applied to the joint. Another is that the solder is applied to a cold joint, making it difficult for the solder to flow properly.

A system that does seem to work quite well it to heavily tin both the end of the lead and the component tag with solder. With the bit also quite heavily tinned, holding the lead in place on the tag and then briefly applying the iron will usually produce a good quality joint. This method may not sound much different to the pouring method that I advised against, and I suppose that the differences are small. They are important though. With this second method you are relying quite heavily on the solder already on the tag and lead. You are basically just using the iron to melt the two areas of solder and merge them into one, with the iron providing little additional solder. With the pouring method you are relying on the iron to provide most of the solder, which simply does not work properly.

With most soldering there is a slight problem in that it requires three hands. One hand to hold the iron, a second to hold the leadout wire, and a third to hold the solder. In practice you will soon devise your own methods of dispensing with the third hand. With point-to-point wiring the most popular method is to form the end of each lead into a simple hook, which can then be hooked around the component tag. Some tags have a hole in the middle, while others are really a form of printed circuit pin and are not primarily intended for point-to-point construction. With either type it is not difficult to hook or bind the lead in position (Figure 2.1), leaving one hand to hold the soldering iron and the other to feed in the solder.

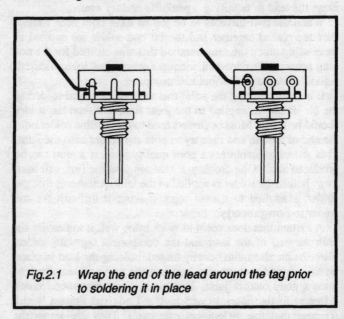

Fig.2.1   Wrap the end of the lead around the tag prior
to soldering it in place

It is important that the lead and tag are kept reasonably still while the solder is setting. With modern solders the setting time is generally quite short, which helps to avoid problems with bad joints due to movement of the objects being soldered.

However, an excessive amount of vibration can still cause problems. A joint that has been affected in this way normally has a rather dull finish instead of the bright finish of a normal joint. In many cases such a joint is so weak mechanically that it is easily pulled apart. If a joint of this type is produced, clean away the old solder and start again.

Like any practical skill, you will not become proficient at soldering by reading about it. The only way to become competent at soldering is to practice until you have acquired the necessary skills. Although many beginners seem to be reluctant to get started as they perceive soldering as being a difficult skill, this is not really the case. Producing really neat soldered joints every time is quite a difficult task, but producing reasonably neat results with reliable connections is really quite straightforward.

I would advise against learning soldering when you commence your first project. It is much better to buy a few components and some wire, and then get in some practice before you start soldering in earnest. Even if the components are wasted, it will still be money well spent. However, there should be no difficulty in removing the leads from the potentiometers, switches, or whatever, so that the components can be reused in projects. Even just banging some panel pins into an odd scrap of fibre board and wiring them together with some 22 s.w.g. tinned copper wire will be good experience and will cost very little.

Board Stiff

Most of the soldering in modern project construction involves fitting small components onto a printed circuit board (p.c.b.). Basically a printed circuit board just consists of a thin but rigid sheet of an insulating material, such as s.r.b.p. or fibreglass. Some modern circuit boards are quite complex affairs, but here we will only consider simple single-sided boards. These have a pattern of copper tracks and pads on one side of the board. There is a small hole (about 0.8 to 1mm diameter) in the middle of each copper pad. Figure 2.2 shows the copper track pattern for a simple printed circuit board.

The components are mounted on the non-copper side of the board, with their leadout wires threaded through the holes in the

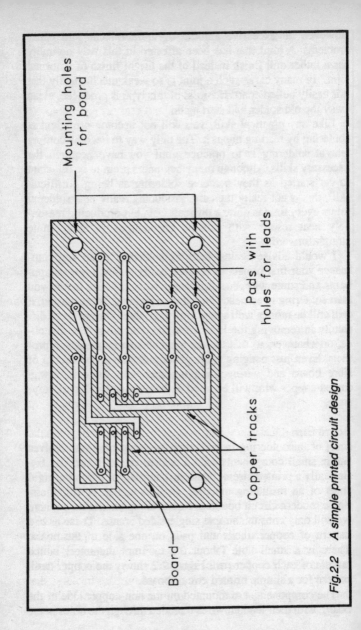

Fig.2.2 A simple printed circuit design

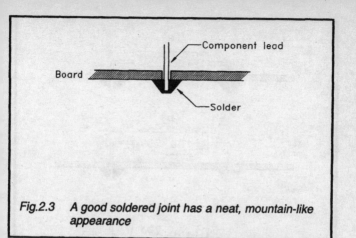

Fig.2.3   *A good soldered joint has a neat, mountain-like appearance*

board. The leads are trimmed on the copper side of the board so that about two or three millimetres of wire is left protruding. The wires are then soldered to the copper pads, and the copper tracks provide the interconnections from one component to the next.

A side-on view of a good printed circuit soldered joint should look something along the lines depicted in Figure 2.3. Here the solder has flowed tightly around the lead and over the copper pad to produce a sort of mountain shape. Apart from providing a good electrical connection, this also provides a secure physical mounting for the component.

It is important that the component is mounted flush with the circuit board, and not raised up slightly (as in Figure 2.4(a)). With the method shown in Figure 2.4(a) there is little risk of any damage to the board if any pressure is placed on the component. The same is not true if there is a gap between the circuit board and the component. Any pressure on the component is not transferred to the top side of the board, but is instead transferred through the leadout wires to the copper pads on the underside of the board. The pads are often quite small, which leaves a real risk of them being pulled away from the board, and they might even be torn away from the copper tracks so that they are no longer in electrical contact with the rest of the circuit. This type of thing is not usually too difficult to repair once

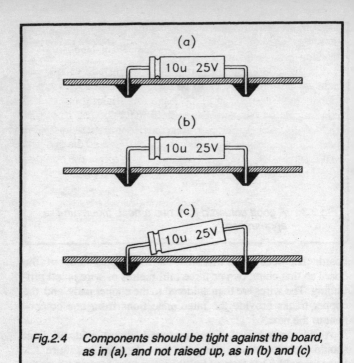

Fig.2.4 Components should be tight against the board, as in (a), and not raised up, as in (b) and (c)

you have spotted the problem, but prevention is better than cure.

Soldering components to a circuit board is not quite as simple as one might think. The first tasks of fitting the components to the board and cutting the leads to length are quite straightforward. However, use proper wire cutters to trim the leads to length. These will give much better results than improvising using scissors or a knife. A good set of wire cutters should only cost a few pounds and should last very many years. Even a cheap pair of combined strippers and cutters are much better than using scissors, and they should have a reasonably long life.

Once the leads have been cut to length there is the problem of completing the soldered joints, and the problem of the third hand. One hand is needed to hold the soldering iron, another is needed to feed in the solder, and at least one more is needed in order to hold the board and component in place. There is more than one way of tackling this problem, and you may well develop your own solutions.

The method I usually adopt when fitting one or two components at a time is to pull out about 300 millimetres or so of solder from the reel, and then leave this sticking out over the edge of the workbench. I then hold the soldering iron in my right hand, and the circuit board and component in my left hand. I then accurately position the board beneath the end of the solder, apply the iron to the joint, and then move the board and iron up into the solder. This may sound like a rather awkward way of handling things, but I find it quite quick and efficient, as do many others. Another popular method is to temporarily glue components in place using Bostik Blu-Tack or Plasticine.

Whatever method you use, make sure that the bit of the iron is applied to the joint first, and that the solder is fed in second. If you do things the other way round it is likely that the solder will not flow properly over the joint. With this type of soldering it is definitely not a good idea to apply the solder to the iron and then pour it onto the joint. Even if the ends of the leadouts wires and the copper pads are generously tinned with solder first, this method is unlikely to give good results. In fact it is more or less guaranteed to produce a large number of bad joints, or "dry" joints as they are often called.

Problems, Problems
There are three likely causes of problems when soldering components onto a printed circuit board, and dry joints are perhaps the most common of these. The normal causes of dry joints (apart from bad soldering technique) are dirt or corrosion on the copper pad or leadout wire. If a pad or leadout is obviously very dirty, it should be cleaned prior to attempting to produce the joint.

If a dry joint is produced it will normally be fairly obvious. The side-on view of a dry joint normally looks similar to Figure 2.5. Rather than the usual mountain shape, the solder tends to form into a globule, and does not flow over the copper pad properly, if at all. The globular shape of a dry joint normally makes its presence readily apparent, as does the mechanical weakness of the joint, which will probably fail to fix the

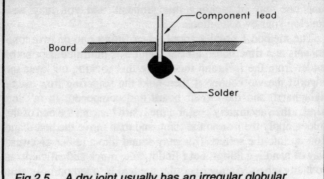

Fig.2.5   A dry joint usually has an irregular globular appearance

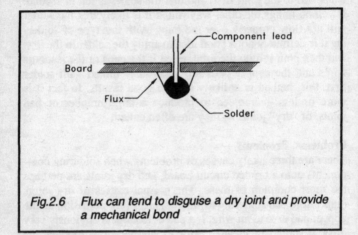

Fig.2.6   Flux can tend to disguise a dry joint and provide a mechanical bond

leadout wire to the pad.

There is a second kind of dry joint, as depicted in Figure 2.6. This can be a little more difficult to spot, as excess flux can provide a reasonably strong mechanical bond, and to some extent disguise the globular shape of the solder. Usually with this type of joint there is no electrical contact between the pad and the leadout wire, making it essential to detect the problem and correct matters.

Usually there is an obvious visual clue to this type of dry joint in the form of large amounts of half-burned flux on and around the joint. Whenever a circuit board becomes heavily contaminated with excess flux it is a good idea to remove it so that you can see if there are any problems lurking underneath. Special cleaning fluids and sprays are available, but I find that the easiest way to remove unwanted flux is to brush it away using something like and old nailbrush or toothbrush. The solder generally has a rather dull finish instead of the usual shiny finish, which again helps to make this type of dry joint stand out. Also, once the flux has been removed it is likely that the globular shape of the solder will be revealed.

The third problem is with excess solder. This can result in the iron leaving a small trail of solder as it is removed from a joint, which can in turn result in unintentional short circuits from one pad to another. Sometimes there is so much excess solder that it is easily spotted, but in other cases the trail of solder is so small that it is difficult to detect visually. You must learn to judge the amount of solder that is needed to produce a strong joint, and then be careful to use no more than this. Be especially careful when working on parts of a board where the tracks and pads are crammed tightly together.

As is the case with point-to-point wiring, movement of the surfaces being joined can result in a poor joint, particularly if the movement occurs while the solder is setting. This is not a common problem when fitting components onto circuit boards though. It is not usually too difficult to hold the components in place on the board, with no movement of the component relative to the board. If this problem should occur, the solder will almost certainly have a dull appearance, and it may actually fracture into numerous tiny pieces.

Practice, Practice

Again, you will not become proficient at soldering components onto printed circuit boards by reading about it. The only way to learn this type of skill is by trying your hand at it, learning from your mistakes, and gaining some experience. It is definitely a good idea to gain some experience before tackling your first project. It is advisable to obtain a small piece of stripboard (a form of proprietary printed circuit board), plus some inexpensive components such as resistors and integrated circuit holders. Alternatively, you might be able to obtain a cheap bargain pack of assorted components. You can then try soldering various bits and pieces to the board. In this way you can rapidly gain some useful experience, and any mistakes made will be of no major consequence. Most people soon get the hang of soldering, and it will become a skill that you can undertake intuitively.

Heat Shunt

One final but important point about soldering is that virtually all electronic components can be damaged by excessive heat from the soldering iron. This makes it important to complete soldered joints reasonably quickly. For small joints it should not be necessary to keep the bit on the joint for more than a second or so.

Modern components are relatively tolerant of heat, but there are a few components that are easily damaged by heat from the soldering iron. Probably the most vulnerable are the various semiconductors, such as transistors, diodes, and integrated circuits. In the case of integrated circuits it is standard practice to fit them onto the board via holders. The holders are soldered to the board, and then the integrated circuits are plugged into the holders. There are no direct soldered connections to the pins of the integrated circuits, and no possibility of these devices being damaged by heat from the iron.

It is possible to use holders for transistors and other semiconductors, but this is not generally deemed to be worthwhile. Simply take a little extra care when soldering transistors, etc., into position. Be especially careful when fitting germanium semiconductors. These days the vast majority of semiconductors are silicon based, but there are still some germanium devices in use. These are mainly germanium diodes, such as the OA90 and OA91.

Some constructors prefer to use a heat shunt on each lead of a vulnerable component as it is soldered in place. Heat shunts vary somewhat in appearance, but they mostly resemble tweezers. The idea is to clip the heat shunt in place on the lead of a component before the lead is soldered to the circuit board.

The heat shunt is fitted onto the leadout wire close to the body of the component. The idea is that much of the heat travelling up the leadout wire towards the body of the component is diverted into the heat shunt. This keeps the component reasonably cool even if the soldering iron is applied to the joint for a few seconds. I have never found it necessary to use a heat shunt, even when fitting germanium diodes to a circuit board. However, if you have difficulty in producing soldered joints reasonably swiftly it might be worthwhile investing in a heat shunt.

Bare Essentials

There are several tools in addition to soldering equipment that should be regarded as essential equipment. Perhaps not everyone would agree, but I regard some form of desoldering tool as an essential item. Apart from the occasional need to remove a component from a printed circuit board, from time to time you will probably want to clean solder away from a bad joint so that a fresh attempt can be made.

Some desoldering tools consist basically of a soldering iron style device to heat the solder to be removed, plus some sort of suction device to actually remove the molten solder. This type of thing tends to be very expensive, since you are effectively buying a second soldering iron. A spring-loaded suction device for use with an ordinary soldering iron is a more economic alternative. There are other ways of removing excess solder, such as desoldering wick, which is used to soak up the molten solder. However, a spring-loaded desoldering tool is the only inexpensive method that I have found to be really effective on a wide range of desoldering jobs.

Screwdrivers are another essential part of the hobby. Probably most households are already equipped with a selection of screwdrivers, but these are likely to be quite large types. Some of these may prove useful for project construction, but you will have to augment them with some small electricians screwdrivers. These are needed for such things as tightening the grub screws on control knobs, and the small fixing screws used for the lids of some project cases. Two or three small screwdrivers should cost very little, and are something you will probably use a great deal. I would recommend buying two flat bladed screwdrivers of different sizes, plus a small crosspoint type.

In many component catalogues you will find sets of miniature "jewellers" screwdrivers. These are very good for camera repairs and the like, but are something I have never found to be particularly useful for project construction. Two or three small electricians screwdrivers are likely to be a much better initial investment.

A hacksaw (or junior hacksaw) and a pair of pliers are further essential items, but will they probably be present in your tool drawer already. Practically any pair of pliers will do, but as one might expect, electrician's pliers are likely to be the most useful in the current context.

Strippers

Plastic insulation can be removed from connecting wire using scissors or a penknife, but I would strongly advise against either method. Improvised methods tend to damage the tool you use, and often involve a strong risk of injuring yourself. They are also ineffective in that they tend to result in slight damage to the wires. Even the slightest of nicks severely weakens the wires, giving a strong risk of the wire breaking before too long.

Even an inexpensive pair of wire strippers (or combined strippers and cutters) should last a long time, and produce good results. Wire strippers have curved cutting blades which can be adjusted so that they cut almost through the insulation, and do not quite reach the wires. The unwanted insulation can then be broken away quite easily, leaving the wires totally undamaged. A pair of wire strippers should be regarded as an essential tool which you will need right from the start.

Hole Truth

Much of the mechanical side of project construction entails drilling holes and making cutouts in cases. It is useful to have a full range of twist drill bits having diameters from about one millimetre to around 10 millimetres. However, initially it is possible to get by with a relatively small number of drills.

Many potentiometers, switches, etc., require a 10 millimetre diameter mounting hole, and a good quality drill bit of this size is something that you will need from the outset. Smaller switches and some sockets require five millimetre or 6.35 millimetre (0.25 inch) diameter mounting holes, and drills of these sizes should also be regarded as indispensable.

Circuit boards can be bolted in place inside the case, or special mountings called stand-offs can be used. Where boards are bolted in place it is usually 6BA or metric M3 fixings that are used. These require mounting holes of about 3.2 or 3.3 millimetres in diameter. The mounting hole requirements of plastic stand-offs vary considerably from one type to another. Initially it is probably best to obtain a 3.2 or 3.3 millimetre diameter drill bit, and use 6BA or M3 fixings. If you eventually start using stand-offs, you can obtain the necessary drill bits at that time.

Drills having diameters of 3.2/3mm, 5mm, 6.35mm, and 10mm are sufficient for constructing most projects, and represent the bare minimum you will need to get started. Before too long you will probably need to add other sizes, such as a 2.6mm drill for small fixing screws (M2.5 or 8BA), and a 4.3mm diameter drill for larger fixing screws (4BA and M4). These additional drill bits can be added as and when they are needed.

With drill bits, as with other tools, there is some advantage in buying high quality types rather than the cheapest you can find. In the main you will probably be drilling holes in relatively soft materials, such as aluminium or plastic. Consequently, inexpensive drills will do the job quite well, and should have a long working life. However, if you opt for inexpensive drill bits, be careful when using the smaller types. Many of these tend to break relatively easily.

When working on projects I generally use a heavy-duty hand drill rather than a power type. The advantage of a hand drill is that it enables you to progress in a controlled manner when drilling into soft materials such as aluminium and plastics. The problem with power drills is that they tend to "snatch", drilling through the work-piece almost instantly. This does not always produce particularly neat results, especially when drilling larger diameter holes. If you use a power drill it should preferably be one that can be set to a slower than normal operating speed. If you have a brace type hand drill, this is likely to be the best choice when drilling larger holes in soft plastics.

Large Holes

Many of the larger switches require a 12.7 millimetre (0.5 inch) diameter mounting hole, which is about the largest size that can be handled using a drill. Even at this size you might prefer to use an alternative, which usually means using a chassis punch (which also known as a chassis cutter). Although relatively few people seem to be familiar with this type of tool, it provides a quick and easy means of producing very high quality holes of around 12.5 to 35 millimetres in diameter.

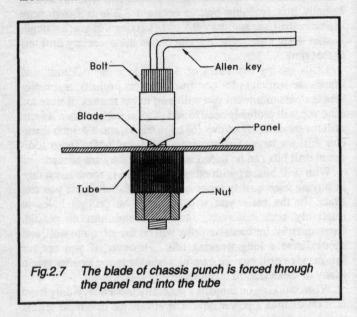

Fig.2.7   The blade of chassis punch is forced through the panel and into the tube

A chassis punch is used in the manner shown in Figure 2.7. It is based on what is essentially just a nut and bolt, and a pilot hole for the bolt must be drilled at the centre of the required cutout. The cutting blade is placed onto the bolt, and the bolt is then pushed into the pilot hole. The nut and a metal tube are placed onto the end of the bolt, and the nut is tightened by hand. An Allen key is then fitted into the bolt, so that the nut and bolt can be tightened further. As the bolt is tightened, it forces the cutting blade through the panel, and down into the tube on the other side of the panel. Eventually the blade is pushed right through the panel and into the tube. This leaves the required hole in the panel, and the nut is then unscrewed so that the whole assembly can be removed from the panel.

Although this may seem to be a crude way of making holes, it actually produces extremely neat results. When large holes are drilled it is normally necessary to do some deburring, but a chassis punch almost invariably leaves a neat and "clean" hole. The only real drawback of chassis punches is their relatively high cost, although good quality punches will last a very long time. Due to their cost it is only worthwhile buying one when you have a definite need for it, and provided you are likely to use it fairly regularly in the future.

Reamers

Reamers provide a relatively low cost alternative to a set of chassis punches. A reamer is a long tapered cutting tool which usually has about five or six cutting blades. Like a chassis punch it requires a pilot hole. It is then placed into the pilot hole and rotated. The larger units often have a built in handle so that they can be rotated by hand, but the smaller types are mostly intended for use in a power or hand drill. As the reamer is rotated, it steadily cuts away at the edge of the hole, making it larger and larger. You just keep cutting until the hole reaches the required size. One slight problem with reamers is that they usually produce rather rough holes that require a fair amount of deburring. Because of this it is advisable to make the hole slightly undersize, to allow for the slight expansion of the hole during the deburring process.

The smaller reamers cover holes from about 3 to 12 millimetres. These provide a useful means of producing odd sized holes that are not covered by your range of drill bits. The larger types cover holes from around 12 to 35 millimetres, and are potentially more useful. They provide a cheap means of producing large holes that are either time consuming or expensive to make using other methods. Unfortunately, the larger reamers are relatively difficult to obtain these days.

Cone cutters are similar to reamers, but they are intended for use in high speed power drills, and file rather than slice the edge of the pilot hole. These are mostly capable of producing their own pilot holes. In general they seem to produce neater results than reamers, but they are quite expensive, and are probably not a practical proposition for most amateur users.

Tanked-Up

A tank cutter can be obtained at relatively low cost, and is a tool that I have found to be very useful for making large circular cutouts up to about 100 millimetres in diameter. I think that I am right in saying that this tool was originally designed for making holes for pipes in water tanks, etc. However, it works well as a general purpose means of making large holes in metal panels and many plastic types.

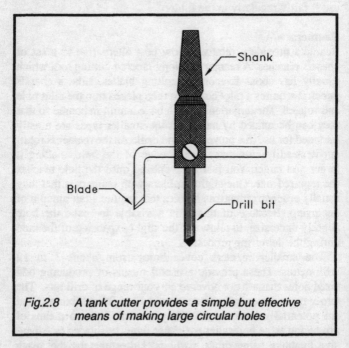

Fig.2.8   A tank cutter provides a simple but effective means of making large circular holes

Figure 2.8 shows the basic way in which this simple tool functions. The cutting blade is set to produce a hole of the required diameter, and then it is locked in place by tightening the screw. With the cutter in position, as it is rotated the blade

74

cuts into the panel, and eventually cuts right through to produce the hole. The cutter must be rotated very slowly, and a fair amount of force is required. Usually this type of tool is only usable in a brace, and not in a normal power or hand drill.

Even large holes can be produced very quickly using a tank cutter. The holes produced have slightly tapered edges, and are not particularly neat. Therefore, it is a good idea to cut the hole slightly too small initially, so that it is brought up to the required size when it is deburred. If you will need to make large round holes to accommodate panel meters, etc., a tank cutter represents what is probably the only cheap and quick means of making the holes.

Getting the Needle

A set of miniature files are more than a little useful, and are something I would recommend you obtain at an early stage. These are useful for deburring, and making adjustments to holes that are not quite the right shape, slightly off-centre, or whatever. A large half-round file is also an extremely useful tool for project construction. If your toolkit does not already include one, it is a good idea to purchase one before starting project construction in earnest.

Most miniature file sets include a round file having a diameter of only about three millimetres or so. A file of this type is often referred to as a "needle" file. A needle file is good for making large cutouts of any size or shape, although even when working on thin aluminium or a soft plastic it is quite a time consuming way of doing things. "Abrafiles" are a popular means of making large cutouts, particularly those that are awkward shapes. The basic "Abrafile" consists of a handle plus a flexible needle file blade that has quite a coarse surface. This enables cutouts to be produced relatively quickly, although it is still quite time consuming to produce larger types. The flexibility of the blade makes it possible to form the blade into shapes that enable it to reach the parts that other files can not reach. However, I have never found this property of much value for project construction.

There is another form of "Abrafile" which looks rather like an outsize junior hacksaw, but the blade is a very thin "needle" file and not a saw blade. The fineness of the blade enables cutouts to be made with relatively high precision. Because the file is in a frame it is possible to exert a comparatively large amount of pressure on it, which together with the small diameter of the file makes it possible to cut at a relatively high rate. This tool probably represents the best way of making large non-circular cutouts. It is probably not worthwhile including it in your toolkit initially, but when you get deeply into project building it will certainly worthwhile buying one of these "Abrafiles."

Coping With Cutouts
The obvious alternative to the frame type "Abrafile" is a coping saw or a fretsaw. Special blades for cutting metal are available, but practically any type of blade will cope with thin aluminium and plastic materials. The fineness of the blade enables a high degree of precision to be achieved if your skills are up to the task. It is quite difficult to make really precise cuts, particularly using a fretsaw which is a rather unwieldy tool. Whenever making large cutouts I would recommend cutting just inside the periphery of the required hole, and then carefully filing it out to precisely the required size and shape.

One slight problem I find when using a fretsaw is that the blades tend to be rather short-lived. This is not due to teeth wearing down, but is a result of them snapping after a small amount of use. For this reason I prefer to use a frame type "Abrafile", even though it is slightly less precise. Another point in favour of an "Abrafile" (or any other form of "needle" file) is that it can cut in any direction. This is often a useful feature, even when making simple cutouts. It is usually an invaluable property when cutting intricate shapes.

Framed
If you find yourself building quite large numbers of printed circuit boards, you might consider buying a printed circuit frame (which is also known as a printed circuit jig amongst other things). These vary somewhat in their exact appearance and method of use, but they all provide the same basic function. Figure 2.9 helps to explain the way in which they operate.

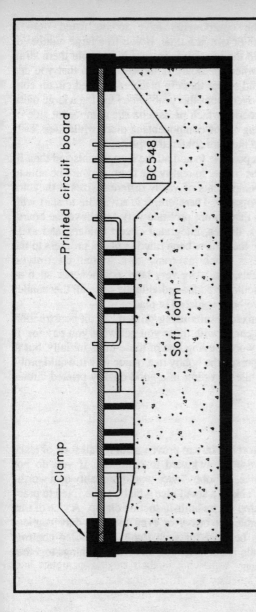

Fig.2.9   A printed circuit frame uses foam and a clamp to hold components in place while they are soldered to the board

Normally the components have to be fitted onto a circuit board one or two at a time. If you fit a large number of components onto the board it is impossible to hold them all in place properly when the board is turned over so that you can trim the leads and solder them in place. A printed circuit construction frame overcomes this problem by having a large piece of soft foam material which presses on the component side of the board, holding all the components in place while their leads are trimmed and they are soldered in place.

In theory it is possible to add all the components and then fit the board into the frame. In reality the foam may not be able to accommodate components of vastly different sizes if they are mounted close together. Therefore, it is advisable to start with the components that do not protrude very far above the board, such as resistors, diodes, integrated circuit holders, and axial capacitors. Once these have been fitted in place, progress to the taller components, such as transistors, radial electrolytic capacitors, crystals, etc. Any very large components, such as transformers, should be added individually once all the smaller components have been soldered in place.

I have had mixed results using printed circuit construction frames, and in general with these you get what you pay for. It is probably not worth buying one of these units initially, but if you eventually pursue the hobby in a major way it would probably be worthwhile investing in a good quality printed circuit frame.

Minor Vice

A vice of some sort is likely to prove useful for all sorts of tasks that will otherwise be awkward to complete. If you do not already have a vice, a "hobby" vice would probably be a worthwhile purchase. This is a small vice which can be fixed to practically any worktop via its built-in suction clamp. A vice of this type is not suitable for heavy or even medium duty applications, but it can be used for such things as holding controls while their spindle is cut to length, and holding things together while the glue sets.

Finally

Ideas on what constitutes a minimal toolkit for constructing simple electronic projects varies from constructor to constructor. This is my suggested tool selection for someone wishing to build a few simple projects.

15 to 20 watt soldering iron and a large reel of 22 s.w.g.
    multi-cored solder
Matching soldering iron stand
Desoldering tool
Three small to medium sized electrician's screwdrivers
    (including one crosspoint type)
Pair of electrician's pliers
Good quality hand or power drill
3.3, 5, 6.35, and 10 millimetre diameter drill bits
Hacksaw or junior hacksaw
Centre punch
Small hammer
Wire cutters
Wire strippers
Penknife
Set of miniature files
Large half-round file
Bostik Blu-Tack or Plasticine

There are other tools that you will need in order to undertake more complex projects, but the exact requirements will depend on the types of projects you build. I would suggest starting with those listed here, and adding others as and when you need them.

Chapter 3

CONSTRUCTION METHODS

These days virtually all electronic devices are based on some kind of circuit board. There are various forms of circuit board, but they are really just variations on a theme. They are all forms of printed circuit board (see chapter 2), or a modification of this idea. There are only two types of circuit board which are currently popular as the basis of electronic projects. These are normal printed circuit boards, and stripboard (a proprietary form of printed circuit board).

There are other methods of construction, such as wire-wrapping and plain matrix board, but these are primarily used for prototyping. However, they will be briefly considered in this chapter, together with surface mount construction, which is another form of printed circuit construction. We will also consider general topics, such as mounting circuit boards, and designing the general layout of a project.

Stripboard
Stripboard has been a popular construction method for a great many years. Like all really good ideas, it is a very simple one. A thin but rigid sheet of an insulating material is drilled with hundreds of holes on a regular matrix. Boards having the holes on various pitches have been produced over the years, but these days only 0.1 inch (2.54 millimetre) board is in large scale use. It is only 0.1 inch pitch board that is available from most component retailers at present. Boards having other pitches are of little use these days, as they will not accept d.i.l. integrated circuits (which have their pins on a 0.1 inch pitch). On one side of the board there are copper strips running along the rows of holes, and each strip runs the full length of the board. Figure 3.1 shows this general scheme of things.

In use stripboard is used in basically the same manner as an ordinary printed circuit board. First the components are fitted on the non-copper side of the board, and then the leadout wires are cropped short. Then the ends of the leadout wires are soldered to the copper strips. The copper strips carry the

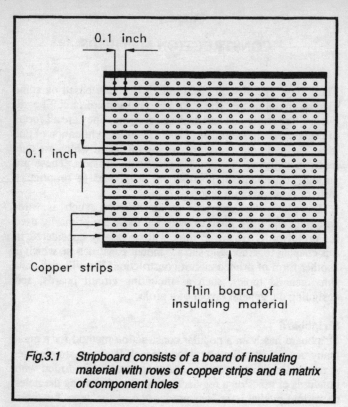

0.1 inch

0.1 inch

Copper strips

Thin board of
insulating material

*Fig.3.1 Stripboard consists of a board of insulating
material with rows of copper strips and a matrix
of component holes*

interconnections between the components.

With a normal printed circuit board the components are
arranged neatly on the board, and the required connections are
provided by what is often a very intricate pattern of copper
tracks. Stripboard construction imposes some compromises,
since the copper strips only provide a very basic method of
interconnection. In practice it is often necessary to use link-
wires to provide connections between strips, and to make
breaks in the copper strips so that each one can handle more
than one set of interconnections. In this way it is possible to
build quite complex circuits on stripboard, but the finished
product is unlikely to be as small and neat as an equivalent
based on a custom printed circuit board.

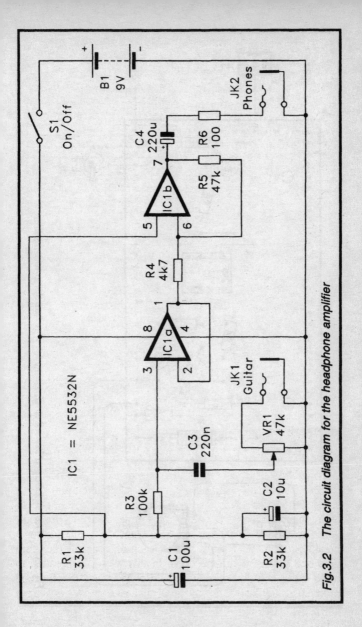

Fig.3.2   The circuit diagram for the headphone amplifier

83

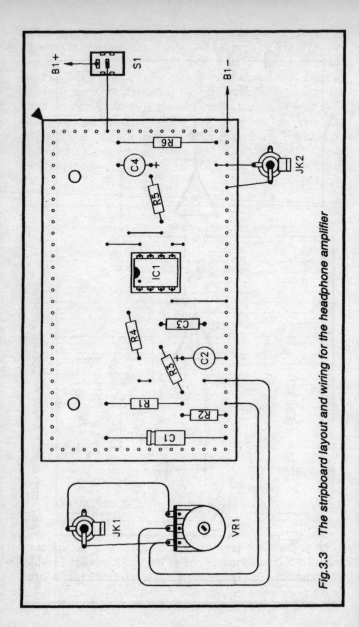

Fig.3.3 The stripboard layout and wiring for the headphone amplifier

84

Headphone Amplifier

A simple example project is probably the best way of showing how stripboard is used, and Figure 3.2 shows the circuit diagram for a simple headphone amplifier for use with an electric guitar. This circuit has been "borrowed" from the book "Practical Electronic Music Projects" (BP363), from the same publisher and author as this publication. BP363 should be consulted if you require information on the way in which this circuit functions, or the way in which the amplifier is used. Figures 3.3 and 3.4 respectively show the component layout and underside view of the board.

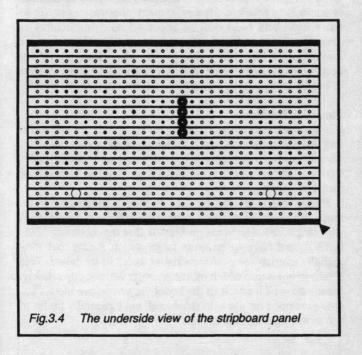

Fig.3.4   The underside view of the stripboard panel

Most published projects, including this one, do not use a piece of stripboard that is one of the standard sizes in which stripboard is sold. Therefore, the first task is to trim a larger board down to the required size. In this case a board having 29 holes by 17 copper strips is required. The board can be cut to size using a hacksaw or junior hacksaw, cutting along rows of holes. Cutting between rows of holes is not a practical proposition because the spacing between the rows of holes is too small. Cutting along rows of holes leaves rather rough edges, but these are easily filed to a smooth finish. It is advisable to proceed quite carefully when cutting and filing stripboard, as some boards are quite brittle and can break if they are treated roughly.

The next task is to make any necessary breaks in the copper strips. In this example only four cuts are needed. A special tool for severing the copper strips is available from most of the larger component retailers. However, many constructors prefer to use a hand-held twist drill of about 4.5 to 5 millimetres in diameter. Either way, always make sure that the strips are broken across their full width. On the other hand, do not cut deeply into the board, especially in cases where a large number of breaks are required. This could severely weaken the board.

Mounting Problems

It is advisable to drill the mounting holes in the board before fitting the components in place. A couple of mounting holes are normally quite sufficient with a small board such as this. Holes having a diameter of 3.3 millimetres are suitable for 6BA or metric M3 fixing screws.

Plastic stand-offs can be used to mount circuit boards on cases, but in my experience most stand-offs do not work well with stripboard. The usual problem is that the mounting holes in the board have to be quite large, which means that they partially overlap some of the existing holes in the board. This results in holes into which most stand-offs will not clip reliably. Stand-offs which attach to the board via screws are more likely to give good results with stripboard, but I generally prefer to use mounting bolts and spacers.

Counting On It

Once the breaks in the strips have been completed and the mounting holes have been drilled, the board is ready for the components and link-wires to be fitted. The precise order in which the components and link-wires are fitted is not usually too important, but the semiconductors are generally the most delicate components. Therefore, it is best to leave the semiconductors until last. Where holders are used, the holders can be added at any stage, but obviously the integrated circuits should not be fitted until the board is otherwise complete. It is advisable to work methodically, or at least semi-methodically, especially with larger boards.

My usual method is to add the integrated circuit holders first, being careful to get them all in the correct place. These then act as guides which make it easier to fit the other components in the right places. With the remaining components and the link-wires I start on the left side of the board and work methodically across to the right. Where large and small components are to be fitted side-by-side it is generally easier if the small components (or link-wires) are added first.

With stripboard it is essential to take great care in order to avoid getting components in the wrong places. Mistakes can usually be corrected without too much difficulty, but correcting a lot of mistakes will soon render the underside of the board a bit of a mess. It is better to proceed carefully, with frequent checking, so that mistakes are to a large extent avoided. Some stripboard layout diagrams have the strips labelled "A", "B", "C", etc., and rows of holes numbered "1", "2", "3", etc. Many constructors find that marking the board with these letters and numbers makes it quicker and easier to find each component mounting hole, and avoids a lot of errors. Some fibre-tip pens will write direct onto the board, or the co-ordinates can be marked onto strips of paper temporarily glued to the top side of the board.

Short link wires can be made from the wires trimmed from resistors and electrolytic capacitors. This is not just an economy measure, and the wire trimmed from these components seems to be ideal for link-wires. For the longer links it is necessary to use 22 or 24 s.w.g. tinned copper wire. I find that the 22 s.w.g. wire is a fraction thicker than would be ideal, and the 24 s.w.g. wire is slightly on the thin side. However, either will do the job quite well, and I usually opt for the thicker gauge.

I have never found it necessary to insulate link-wires with p.v.c. sleeving, even where there are several long wires running side-by-side. However, they must be kept quite taut so that a reliable gap is maintained between the wires. I start by cutting a slightly over-length piece of wire, and then solder one end to the board at the appropriate hole. Then I thread the wire through the other hole, and use a pair of pliers to pull it tight enough to straighten out the wire between the two holes. This forms the wire into the required shape, and it holds this shape while the free end of the wire is trimmed to length and soldered to the board.

Solder Pins

Leads from any controls, sockets, etc., can simply be soldered direct to the board. This is not a very good way of doing things though, and I would definitely advise against it. The main problem with the direct method is that any twisting of the leads tends to tear the tracks away from the board, as does any pressure on the lead near the connection to the board.

It is much better to make the connections to the board via solder pins. For 0.1 in pitch stripboard it is one millimetre (0.04 inch) diameter pins that are required. In most cases it is single-sided pins that are needed, and these are used in the manner shown in Figure 3.5.

The pin is inserted from the underside (copper side) of the board. A pin insertion tool is available, but there is normally little difficulty in fitting the pins by hand. However, make sure that every pin is fully pushed into place, and if necessary use pliers to fully push home each one. Once in place the pins are soldered to the board in the usual way, but use plenty of solder. After tinning the top of the pin and the end of the lead with solder, there should be no difficulty in joining the two. Twist the end of the leadout wire around the pin, and then apply the bit and feed in some solder. Again, use plenty of solder to ensure that a strong joint is produced.

Double-sided pins (Figure 3.6) are only needed when it is necessary to make connections to both the top and bottom sides of the board. In most cases this is not necessary, but in some cases the circuit board is mounted in the middle of the case, effectively dividing it in two, with off-board components mounted either side of the board. Double-sided pins then offer the neatest means of making the off-board connections. Double-side pins tend to be more difficult to fit into place, but

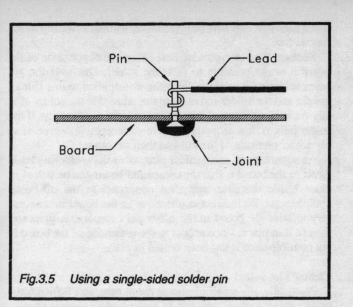

Fig.3.5   Using a single-sided solder pin

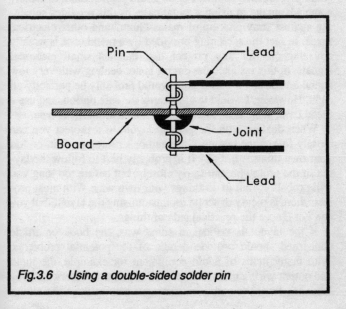

Fig.3.6   Using a double-sided solder pin

it is a task that can still be undertaken without resorting to the special tool.

Because the pin protrudes well below the copper side of the board it is not possible to flow the solder right over the pin when soldering it in place. With the iron applied to one side of the pin and the solder fed in from the other side the solder usually flows nicely around the pin and over the copper strip. If the solder fails to flow around the pin to an acceptable degree, simply solder one side of the pin and then the other.

An advantage of using solder pins rather than soldering leads direct to the board is that the completed board can be bolted in place inside the case, and then connected to the off-board components. With direct connections to the board it is necessary to wire the board to the off-board components first, and then fit it in place, since access to the underside of the board is not possible once it has been bolted in place.

Casing The Joints

Practically any small plastic or metal case will suffice for a small project such as this. For an audio project there is usually some advantage in using a metal case, as this provides screening against stray pick-up of mains "hum" and other electrical noise. In fact the screening provided by a metal case is usually advantageous for any project that handles small electrical signals. In this instance the circuit is not dealing with very low signal levels, and a plastic case would probably be perfectly all right. However, I would tend towards the safe option, and use a metal case, such as an inexpensive folded aluminium type.

When dealing with the general layout of a project you can closely follow the layout of the author's prototype unit, or "do your own thing." Initially it is probably best to follow the layout of the prototype unit fairly closely, but before too long you will probably want to do things your own way. With most projects there is plenty of scope for customising the layout, but you can not ignore the practical side of things.

If the layout is critical in some way, the book or article concerned should provide details of the potential problems. With many items of audio equipment for example, the input and output wiring must be kept well separated. Otherwise stray feedback from the output to the input can result in the circuit

90

oscillating, or some less severe form of instability. The gain of this amplifier is not very high, and a small amount of stray feedback via the input and output wiring is not likely to have any major consequence. Even so, it is probably better to play safe and keep the input and output wiring well apart.

When designing front panel layouts I usually place the control knobs on the panel, and move them around to find a pleasing arrangement. If there are sockets, toggle switches, etc., to contend with, use the fixing nuts to represent these on the mock-up front panel. If necessary, Bostik Blu-Tack or Plasticine can be used to help hold everything in place.

Spaced-Out

Using this method you should soon arrive at a neat layout, but it is as well to check for possible problems before drilling the holes in the case. A common mistake is to have some of the controls too close together. Remember that the control on the rear of the panel might be larger than the control knob on the front. It is particularly important to check that you have left enough space for larger controls, such as rotary switches.

Are there any obstructions on the inside of the case that you have overlooked? Apart from the circuit board, battery, etc., there may well be obstructions in the case itself. There may be unused mounting pillars for the board. Mounting pillars are fine if you can make use of them, but in most cases they will not be apposite to the board you are using, and they may well get in the way. Fortunately, in most cases they can be carefully drilled away. There are often pillars that take the mounting screws for the lid of the case, and these often seem to be out of all proportion to the screws that fit into them. Will these obstruct any of the components mounted on the front panel? Metal cases often have a lid or cover that is fixed by two or four self-tapping screws. These screws can be quite long, and layouts must be carefully designed to leave clear spaces for them.

Once you have found a neat and acceptable layout, carefully measure the position of every component on the front panel, and write down the measurements on a piece of paper. It is not essential to draw up a neat plan of the front panel, but make sure that the exact position of everything on the panel is noted down. At this stage you should also check that nothing has been overlooked. It is all to easy to complete the drilling of a panel and then discover that a l.e.d., socket, or whatever has been completely overlooked. It is usually possible to find a space for a minor front panel component, but the symmetry and general balance of the layout will almost certainly be compromised. If a major component (potentiometer, switch, etc.) is overlooked, it may be necessary to discard the case and start again.

Making Your Mark

The final layout must be marked onto the front panel as accurately as possible. Fibre-tipped pens which have a spirit based ink will mark most aluminium and plastic panels, and the marks are easily washed off once the drilling has been completed. Soft pencils are also usable on aluminium, but only press very gently or scratches might be left when the pencil marks are rubbed off.

As an alternative to marking the panel directly, you can paste a sheet of paper onto the panel, and then mark the positions of the holes onto this. Once the drilling has been completed the panel is soaked in water, and the paper and paste are then easily cleaned off. This method is obviously a bit more time consuming than directly marking the panel, but in my experience it generally gives the most accurate results. Also, the paper covering gives the panel a certain amount of protection against accidental scratches while the drilling is being carried out.

When working on aluminium a centre punch should be used to make an indentation at the centre of each proposed hole. This acts as a guide for the drill bit, which might otherwise tend to wander instead of staying properly centred. A centre punch will work properly with some plastics, and is generally satisfactory with the softer types. It will require relatively little force to make each indentation though. With harder plastics there is a real risk of the panel cracking, and a centre punch should therefore not be used with hard plastics. Gentle pressure from a bradawl or a similar pointed tool will usually give an adequate indentation when working on harder plastics.

With small holes of up to about four millimetres in diameter it is satisfactory to drill them full size first time. With larger holes it is generally better if a small pilot hole about 2.5 to three millimetres in diameter is drilled first, and this is then drilled out to the required size. Where possible it is better if the panel is clamped onto a scrap piece of timber or particle board, rather than having empty space on the underside of the panel. This avoids having the drill suddenly crash down through the completed hole, and should also give a "cleaner" hole.

It is likely that a small amount of deburring will still be needed though. With soft materials such as aluminium and plastics I find that the small blade of a penknife provides a quick and easy means of deburring larger holes. With small holes a hand-held twist drill bit of a substantially larger diameter provides a very speedy means of deburring even the roughest of holes.

Mounting Tension

When a circuit board is mounted inside a metal case it is essential that the underside of the board is kept well clear of the case. Otherwise the connections on the underside of the board will be short circuited through the metal case. It is not strictly necessary to space the board from a plastic case, since plastic is an excellent insulator. However, I would still advise spacing boards at least a few millimetres off the case.

The reason for this is simply that the underside of a circuit board is far from flat, due to the soldered joints protruding on this side of the board. If you simply bolt the board to the case without using any spacers, this tends to distort the board, as in Figure 3.7. Some stripboards are quite brittle, and this could result in the board cracking. Even if the board does survive intact, it will be left under a fair amount of tension, and might fail at some later time.

This problem can be avoided by using some spacers or additional nuts over the mounting bolts, between the case and the board, as shown in Figure 3.8. There are two types of spacer, which are the threaded and plain varieties. Either type is suitable for this application, but the threaded variety are the easier to use, as with these it is not necessary to hold everything carefully in position while the two fixing nuts are put into place.

The mounting holes in the case must be drilled to accurately match the holes in the board, or the board may tend to buckle

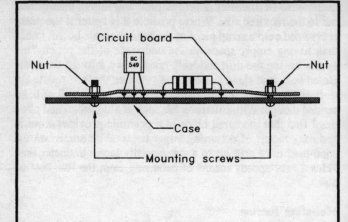

Fig.3.7 Simply bolting a circuit board in place can distort and damage it

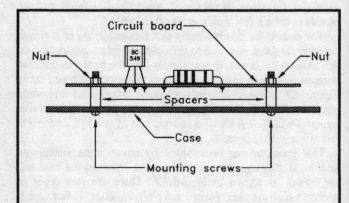

Fig.3.8 Using spacers to keep the underside of the circuit board clear of the case

and crack as the mounting nuts are tightened. I find that the best method of marking the positions of the mounting holes on the panel is to use the board itself as a sort of template.

In Control

Drill the holes for the controls, sockets, etc., before finally fitting the circuit board in the case. Potentiometers and rotary switches have quite long spindles, and they are designed to be used with "dummy" front panels. This arrangement is shown in Figure 3.9. In this example the controls are mounted on the "dummy" panel which is fitted behind the real front panel. There is an alternative which has the controls mounted on the front panel of the case, with the "dummy" panel added just ahead of the real panel. This second method is not applicable to many types of case.

The point of these "dummy" panels is to allow the control knobs to fit almost right against the panel, so as to give a neat appearance. Although "dummy" panels are commonplace on ready-made equipment, they are little used by home constructors. With many projects a system of this type would be difficult to implement, and would probably not be worth the considerable effort involved. Even where a "dummy" panel could be used without too much difficulty, it is easier to use recessed control knobs. Most control knobs over about 20 millimetres in diameter are of this type, and are designed to fit over the control's mounting nut and bush (Figure 3.10). This enables the knob to effectively fit virtually flush with the front panel without having to resort to any form of "dummy" front panel.

Unless you want the control knobs to look as though they are on stalks, the spindles of the controls must be trimmed to a suitable length. For most control knobs a spindle length of about 10 millimetres or so is suitable. Plastic and metal spindles can be trimmed using a hacksaw or junior hacksaw. Hold the spindle in a vice while it is cut using the saw. Do not clamp the control in the vice. Apart from the fact that this would leave the spindle free to rotate while you try to saw through it, clamping the control in a vice could seriously damage the component.

The end of the spindle will probably be left with a slightly rough finish, but this can be cleaned up using a small flat file.

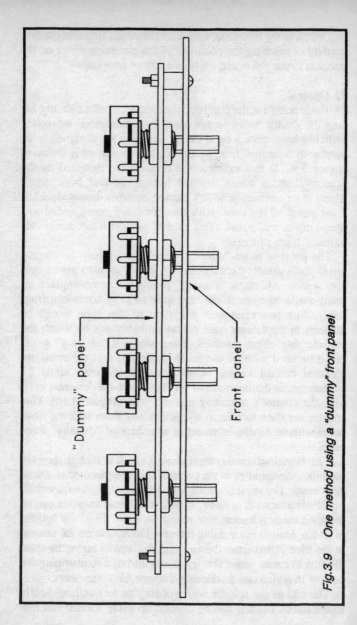

Fig.3.9   One method using a "dummy" front panel

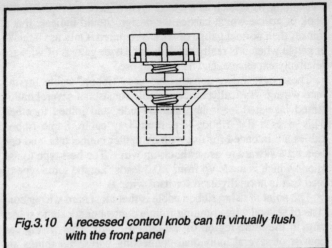

Fig.3.10 A recessed control knob can fit virtually flush with the front panel

Most plastic spindles can be almost instantly cut to length using a large pair of wire clippers. Again, this will probably leave a slightly rough end, but a little filing will soon restore a neat end that will fit into the control knob without difficulty.

End of the Rainbow

Soldering connecting wires to controls, sockets, printed circuit pins, etc., was covered in chapter 2, and we will not cover the same ground again here. It is perhaps worth making the point that the correct type of wire is a multi-strand p.v.c. insulated type. Single-strand connecting wire is available, and has potential advantages in some applications, such as where a large number of wires are to be combined in a large cable-form. This type of thing is rare in projects for the home constructor, and for general wiring work single-strand wire lacks flexibility, and more prone to snapping.

Most component catalogues provide a choice of several multi-strand connecting wires, or "hook-up" wires as they are often called. For general use a 7/0.2 wire (i.e. seven cores of wire 0.2 millimetres in diameter) is probably the best choice. Projects which involve high currents, such as bench power supplies and power amplifiers, may require a heavier gauge of connecting wire, such as a 24/0.2 type. Where appropriate, the book or article which carries the design should indicate that a thicker than normal gauge of wire is required. Only use a thicker gauge when it is really needed, as heavier gauges of wire are relatively expensive, and difficult to use.

These days many constructors use "ribbon" cable for the hard wiring. Basically, a ribbon cable consists of several multistrand insulated leads laid side-by-side, and joined together. This gives a flat, ribbon-like, multi-way cable. Some ribbon cables are intended for use with computer connectors, and can be a bit awkward to use as hook-up wires. The best type to use is one which is made up from 7/0.2 leads (i.e. the same type of lead that is normally used for hard wiring).

The point of using ribbon cable is that most hard wiring consists of several wires running from a control or socket to solder pins in the same region of the circuit board. This wiring can consist of several individual connecting wires, but things are generally easier and neater if a piece of ribbon cable is used. Ribbon cable is normally sold in 10, 20, and 30 way sizes, but for most hard wiring the 10 way variety is perfectly adequate. If a large number of interconnections are required it is usually easier to split them up into two or three cables, rather than one monster cable having about 12 to 30 leads.

In most cases far less than 10 way cable will be needed, but it is easy to peel off a cable having the required number of ways. This type of ribbon cable is designed to pull apart relatively easily. Ribbon cable intended for hard wiring usually has a different colour for each lead, and it is often referred to as "rainbow" ribbon cable. Having each lead a different colour reduces the risk of mistakes with crossed over wires. Also, if a mistake should be made it is comparatively easy to spot it and correct the error.

Hard Wiring

The wiring to the controls, etc., has various names, such as "point-to-point", "spaghetti", and "hard" wiring. This last name is quite appropriate because the hard wiring is relatively difficult, and the beginner is more likely to run into difficulties with this wiring than when fitting components onto the circuit board!

Initially, I would strongly recommend that projects are only built from a book or magazine that provides full construction information, including a wiring diagram. Once you have gained some experience at project building you will probably wish to build a few designs working direct from a circuit diagram. For small to medium size projects this is not too difficult, but it is not the place to start.

With the aid of a wiring diagram, such as Figure 3.3 for this example project, it is reasonably easy to get all the interconnections right first time. There is a physical representation of each off-board component, making it fairly obvious which two points each lead connects to. There is a possible catch in that some components are available in two or more physical styles. For example, many jack sockets are available in metal open construction form, and in a plastic insulated form. Figure 3.3 shows JK1 as an open construction type, which is the most common form for 3.5 millimetre jack sockets.

The experienced constructor usually has little difficulty in sorting out the connections to a component which is physically somewhat different to the type illustrated in a wiring diagram. Matters are more difficult for beginners, and where possible I would recommend buying sockets, etc., that are identical to those used in the author's prototype.

This is another example of a large component catalogue proving to be a worthwhile investment. The large component retailers offer a wide choice of sockets, switches, etc., so that you can select precisely the required type, rather than having to settle for a near equivalent. Also, if it should be necessary to use an equivalent, component catalogues often provide connection information that should help to get the substitute component connected correctly.

Printed Circuit Boards

Having looked at the construction of a simple stripboard project we will now consider the same project built using other types of circuit board. The main alternative to stripboard is a custom printed circuit board. Ready-made printed circuit boards are available for many of the projects published in electronics magazines, although in most cases the boards are only available for a few years after each project is published. If a ready-made board is not available it is possible to make your own provided the book or article includes an accurate (preferably life-size) diagram of the copper pattern.

Making your own printed circuit boards is not particularly difficult, but it is a process that goes beyond the scope of this book. Do-it-yourself printed circuit board construction is covered in a separate book ("How To Design And Make Your Own PCBs", BP121), from the same publisher and author as this publication. If you eventually decide to try your hand at making printed circuit boards, BP121 covers simple and photographic methods of producing good quality boards. However, initially I would advise against making your own boards. The first time project builder has a number of new skills to master, and things to learn. Adding to the problems by building your own printed circuit board is probably not a sensible idea.

For your first project there is a lot to be said in favour of using a ready-made custom printed circuit board. A board of this type is likely to be more expensive than using stripboard or a home-made printed circuit board, but it makes construction very straightforward indeed. With stripboard there are large numbers of unused holes, which makes it relatively easy to get a component in the wrong place.

A custom printed circuit board has one hole per leadout wire, which greatly reduces the chances of making an error. Many ready-made boards have a component layout diagram printed on the top side of the board, which makes it even easier to get everything in the right place. If a mistake should be made, it usually becomes pretty obvious before too long, and most errors are easily rectified. Using a custom printed circuit board does not guarantee perfect results every time, but it certainly maximises your chances of getting the project to work properly first time.

Figures 3.11 and 3.12 respectively show the component layout/wiring and copper track pattern for the printed circuit version of the headphone amplifier. I have not made-up and tested this board incidentally, so I can not guarantee that it will work satisfactorily in practice. It is included merely to illustrate the difference between a stripboard and a custom printed circuit board.

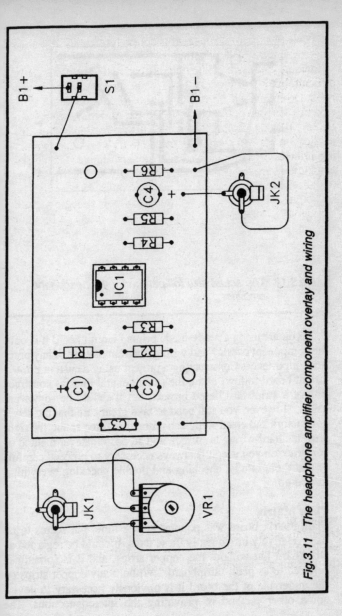

Fig. 3.11 The headphone amplifier component overlay and wiring

101

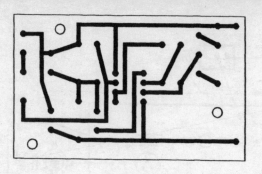

Fig.3.12 The actual size foil pattern for the headphone
amplifier p.c.b.

If you are using a ready-made printed circuit board it is only
the component overlay and wiring diagram that are of any practical importance. Constructing a project using a custom printed
circuit board follows along the same general lines as construction of a stripboard based project, but it should be somewhat
easier. However, you still need to take great care that the semiconductors and electrolytic capacitors are fitted round the right
way, the hard wiring is correct, and so on. Whatever method of
construction you use, it is always necessary to proceed carefully and thoughtfully, checking and double checking everything
as you go.

Plain Matrix
Plain matrix board was popular at one time, but seems to be
used relatively infrequently these days. It could be regarded as
stripboard but without the copper strips, and it is sometimes
referred to as plain "stripboard." Without any copper strips on
the underside of the board it is obviously necessary to devise
some other method of providing the interconnections. The

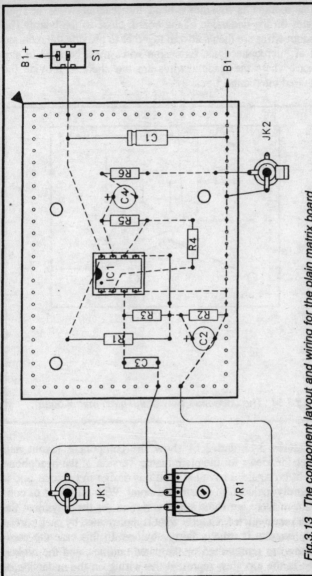

Fig.3.13 The component layout and wiring for the plain matrix board

usual method is to simply bend the leadout wires at right angles on the underside of the board, close to the board. The leadout wires are then soldered together to provide the required set of interconnections. Extension wires must be used in any places where the leadout wires are too short to provide the required interconnections.

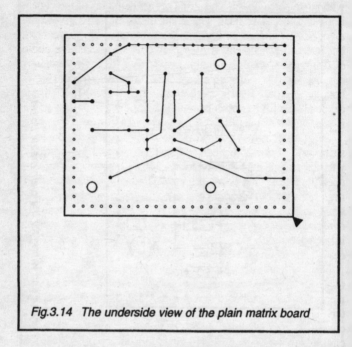

Fig.3.14 The underside view of the plain matrix board

Figures 3.13 and 3.14 show the component layout and underside views for the plain matrix version of the headphone amplifier. Again, I have not tried this design in practice, and it is merely included to illustrate a point. With all forms of construction there are some slight variations in the ways that the boards are depicted. Exactly what is represented by each part of each diagram is usually fairly obvious. In this case the components are represented by the usual outlines, and the broken lines in the top view represent the wiring on the underside of the board. The solid lines in the underside view also represent the wiring.

Although this method of construction tends to be regarded as a bit old fashioned, it does have one or two advantages. Probably the most important of these is that it provides a universal construction method like stripboard, but without the capacitance between the copper strips that can be problematic when using stripboard. The strips act as the plates of the capacitors, and the board itself acts as the dielectric. This gives only a very small amount of capacitance from one strip to the next, but it can be sufficient to give problems with sensitive audio circuits, and it can give major problems with high frequency circuits such as radio receivers. Like custom printed circuit boards, the plain matrix method of construction gives minute capacitances from one set of interconnections to another, and it is well suited to many high frequency applications.

Another point in favour of plain matrix board compared to stripboard is that it permits the use of vertical connections, whereas stripboard can only accommodate horizontal interconnections unless link-wires are used. This often enables rather neater and more compact component layouts to be used. It is also possible to have wires which cross over without actually coming into electrical contact, provided at least one of the wires is insulated with p.v.c. sleeving. Again, this makes it possible to devise more compact component layouts.

The only real drawback of plain matrix board is that it is relatively slow and cumbersome to use. Most constructors find it easier to use stripboard or a custom printed circuit board, and this has resulted in a decline in the popularity of plain matrix construction. For those who like to experiment with radio circuits it remains an excellent basis for prototype circuits.

There is a variation on the plain matrix method of construction which is based on an non-drilled s.r.b.p. board. The constructor drills the board with component holes at the appropriate places, and then construction proceeds in the normal fashion. If done well this gives a neater finished product than a board based on plain matrix board. In fact, from the component side it should look just like a custom printed circuit board. This method of construction is far from popular though, and most constructors seem to prefer the relative ease with which plain matrix board can be used.

Surface Mount

Despite many predictions that surface mount boards would dominate the world of electronics by the end of the 1980s, by the mid 1990s this has not really happened. Surface mount technology is excellent where quite large production runs are required, as it enables the boards to be produced using automatic production methods. This enables complex circuit boards to be produced relatively cheaply. Although it makes automatic production very easy, it makes life more difficult for one-off projects or short production runs where boards must be built by hand.

A few surface mount projects for home constructors have appeared in recent years, and it seems likely that a lot more will follow. One reason for this is that some new semiconductors are only produced in surface mount versions. It is actually possible to obtain converters that effectively turn a surface mount integrated circuit into a conventional d.i.l. type. The problem with these converters is that they are intended for use by professionals when developing circuits using surface mount devices, and they too expensive for use in projects. Using surface mount construction, or a combination of conventional printed circuit and surface mount construction are generally more satisfactory solutions to the problem.

Surface mount construction is really just another variation on the conventional printed circuit board. The most obvious difference between a surface mount board and a normal printed circuit board is that the components are mounted on the copper side of the board. Also, there are no holes for the component leadouts and pins, because surface mount components do not have conventional leadout wires and pins.

Integrated circuits and some other semiconductors have encapsulations that look rather like miniature versions of conventional d.i.l. devices, but with about half the pin spacing (i.e. around 0.05 inches instead of 0.1 inches). However, closer inspection shows that the pins are really small tabs, rather like small wings that stick out sideways from the body of the component. They are not bent through right angles like the pins of a normal integrated circuit. The normal form of most resistors, capacitors, and other simple components is a box shape, with overall dimensions that are often only about one, by two by

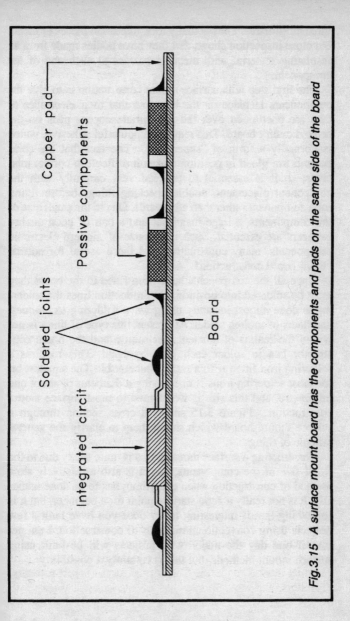

Fig.3.15 A surface mount board has the components and pads on the same side of the board

three millimetres. They actually look like small pieces of metal, but close inspection shows that they have bodies made from an insulating material with metal electrodes at each end of the component.

The first step with surface mount construction is to glue the components in place on the board so that their electrodes or tabs are positioned over the appropriate copper pads on the printed circuit board. This requires a powerful adhesive, which is normally a form of "superglue". The fact that the components are glued in position makes it difficult to correct mistakes, so it is essential to proceed very carefully with the component placement, double checking things before fitting each component rather than afterwards. Due to the small size of the components, a large magnifier and a pair of good quality tweezers are essential. Such is the size of modern electronic components, many constructors find these useful for normal circuit board construction!

Once all the components have been fitted to the board they must be soldered into position. On production lines the soldering is done almost instantly using wave soldering techniques, and baths of molten solder. At present this type of thing is not within the realms of amateur electronics, and the home constructor has to solder each joint by hand. This requires a soldering iron fitted with a small diameter bit. The smallest bit for most soldering irons is one having a diameter of about one millimetre, and this size is well suited to most surface mount construction. Figure 3.15 shows a cross section through a surface mount board which should help to clarify the general scheme of things.

Constructing a surface mount board is quite tricky due to the small size of the components, and it is also a relatively slow method of construction when everything has to be done manually. It is not really a good starting point for a beginner, but it is something that is interesting to try once you have built a few projects using conventional methods of construction. I am not sure if one day the majority of projects will be built using surface mount methods, but this is certainly a possibility.

Seeing Double

The conventional and surface mount printed circuit boards described so far are single-sided types. In other words, there are only copper tracks and pads on one side of the board. The problem with single-sided boards is that there are some circuits that can not be accommodated. Sometimes a track from point A to point B is not possible as there are one or more tracks between these two points. It is not possible to run one track over another without having a connection between the two tracks. Some link-wires on the top side of the board can be used if there are only a moderate number of tracks which can not be accommodated by a single-sided board. A link-wire effectively takes a track onto the top side of the board where it can cross over other tracks without connecting to them.

A double-sided board is really just an extension of the link-wire idea, but instead of using wires on the top side of the board, there are copper tracks. The copper tracks on the top and bottom sides of the board must be interconnected, and these connections are provided by holes through the board plus pads on both sides of the board. Some double-sided boards are through-plated, which simply means that the pads on the top and bottom sides of the board are interconnected during the manufacturing process. If a board is not through-plated, the through-board connections must be provided using special pins, which are effectively shorter versions of ordinary single-sided solder pins.

Initially you are unlikely to use a double-sided printed circuit board as these are mainly used for highly complex projects. If you progress to more complex projects it is highly likely that you will use one of these boards, but building single and double-sided boards is broadly similar. When using a through-plated board there is no difference at all. The only difference when using a board that is not through-plated is that you then have the additional pleasure of putting in what may well be a hundred or more through-pins, and then soldering them on both sides of the board. Incidentally, surface-mount boards are almost invariably of the double-sided variety. In some cases they are truly double-sided, with copper tracks and components on both sides of the board.

Wrapping-Up

Wire wrapping is form of construction that it is difficult to describe without a great deal of generalisation. If you ask half a dozen electronic engineers to describe the wire-wrapping process you are quite likely to get half a dozen similar but significantly different descriptions! The problem is that several wire-wrapping systems have been marketed over the years, with each one offering a slightly different approach to this method of construction.

The basic idea is the same for each system. The components are fitted onto some form of matrix board, and they are usually soldered in place, although solderless wire-wrap systems have been produced. The connections between the components are then provided via pieces of very thin wire, and in most cases the wire is insulated by a thin layer of plastic. The wire is contained in a pen-like tool which has a spool of wire at the top end, and the wire coming out the bottom (pointed) end.

With one system the wire is wrapped around the ends of the component pins and leadout wires, and then soldered to them through the insulation on the wire. The insulation is a special type which does not produce any unpleasant or poisonous fumes when it is burnt away by the heat of the iron. With another system each pin and leadout wire is connected via the circuit board to a special form of solder pin. It is these pins that are used when using the wire-wrap pen to provide the interconnections. The pins are designed to cut through the insulation on the connecting wire, so that no soldering is needed when undertaking the wire-wrapping. Yet another system has non-insulated wire in the "pen", which renders soldering optional, but means that insulation has to be added where two or more wires cross over each other.

Wire-wrapping is mainly used by electronic engineers when producing prototype equipment. It enables complex circuits to be rapidly built and tested, and any necessary modifications or corrections can soon be implemented. The problem with this method of construction is that it is relatively difficult to copy the prototype, and as a result of this it is little used for home constructor projects.

Zapping Components

When you start buying components and building electronic projects you will soon start to encounter warnings about "zapping" components with static electricity. With a few possible exceptions, it is only semiconductors that are in danger from being "zapped" by static charges. When you buy some semiconductors you may well find they are supplied in packing that is printed with dire warnings about the consequences of getting the components anywhere near a large static charge. So what are the real dangers of accidentally "zapping" integrated circuits, transistors, and other semiconductors?

The components which are most at risk are MOSFETs (but not Jfets), and integrated circuits that are based on MOS technology. MOS integrated circuits are far more common than discrete MOSFETs, and you are most likely to encounter static-sensitive components in the form of CMOS logic integrated circuits, complex digital integrated circuits such as computer chips, and some linear integrated circuits such as the CA3130E and CA3140E operation amplifiers.

MOSFETs are vulnerable due to their ultra-high input resistances, which are generally in excess of one million megohms! With most components there is no risk of static build-up, because resistances within the component will leak away the charge much faster than it can build up. With MOS inputs this does not occur, because the leakage currents are incredibly small. Static charges can therefore build up until quite a high voltage is reached (possibly a few hundred volts or more), and then the input breaks down causing irreparable damage to the device.

It is now recognised that non-MOS semiconductors can also be damaged by static charges. The problem is not one of a steady build-up of the charge, but is more one of a sudden charge being encountered. This results in a short but large flow of current which can damage semiconductors. In particular, many of today's integrated circuits contain the equivalent of thousands of components, and the individual components are physically extremely small. In normal use the transistors and other components normally handle minute currents, which makes their small physical size perfectly acceptable. However, if a fault condition or a static discharge results in a sudden surge of current, the components can "blow" like tiny fuses.

Protection Racket

In practice the risk of damaging components due to static charges is probably not that great, but the risk is a real one. One obvious precaution is to simply keep semiconductors well away from any obvious source of static charges. This means television sets, computer monitors, carpets that are know to give problems with static, and perhaps even your cat or dog! Also, when handling semiconductors do not wear clothes that are likely to produce static charges. In general it is man-made fibres that are the main risk, with natural fibres such as cotton and wool being completely safe.

These days few garments seem to be made from 100% man-made fibres, and clothes that are made from a mixture of natural and man-made fibres seem to be reasonably free from static. This means that there is relatively little chance of your latest component purchases being "zapped" by your clothes, but it might be as well to check that you have no garments that are 100% polyester, nylon, or whatever.

These are the minimum of precautions which should be taken when dealing with static-sensitive transistors and integrated circuits. First and foremost, leave the integrated circuits in their anti-static packing until it is time to fit them into place. This packing will usually be either a transparent plastic tube, or some form of conductive foam material. The purpose of the tubing is to insulate the pins from high static voltages. The conductive foam effectively places a short circuit across all the pins so that they will all be at the same voltage. Remember that it is a high voltage difference across two pins that is needed in order to "zap" a static-sensitive component, and not just a high voltage per se. Some integrated circuits are now supplied in blister packs which have metal foil to short circuit the pins, and the plastic blister to provide insulation. A sort of "belt and braces" approach to the problem.

Do not fit the integrated circuits into place until the unit is finished in all other respects. It is a good idea to use holders for any d.i.l. integrated circuits, but they should be regarded as mandatory for static-sensitive types. It might occasionally be necessary to directly solder a static-sensitive device to a circuit board. This is most likely to occur when dealing with discrete MOS transistors. Only use a soldering iron having an earthed bit. These days virtually all soldering irons have an earthed bit, but if in doubt you can resort to the alternative of unplugging the iron from the mains prior making the connections. The iron should stay hot long enough to complete at least half a dozen joints.

Once a device has been removed from its protective packing it should be handled as little as possible. It is sometimes suggested that static-sensitive integrated circuits should be fitted into their holders without the pins being touched. This is rather unrealistic, because most d.i.l. integrated circuits require a fair amount of "friendly persuasion" before they will fit into their holders properly. However, it makes sense not to touch the pins any more than is really necessary.

If you wish to take more comprehensive precautions there are various anti-static aids available. These include wrist bands which you can use to earth yourself, and conductive work surfaces (which are also earthed in normal use). Being realistic about it, the cost of many MOS semiconductors is so low that, for the home constructor at any rate, the cost of anti-static equipment is likely to be many times greater than any cost savings it might produce. These anti-static gadgets are perhaps more attractive for commercial users, and (possibly) experimenters who will need to handle MOS devices a good deal. However, having experimented with hundreds of MOS integrated circuits I can not honestly say that I have ever found such gadgets necessary.

Speakers

To finish this chapter we will consider one or two awkward components that are worthy of special mention. We will start with miniature loudspeakers. These are not used quite as much as in the past, with ceramic resonators having taken over in many applications where miniature loudspeakers would once have been used. They are still to be found in a fair number of home-constructor projects though.

Do not waste time looking for the mounting holes in miniature loudspeakers, because they are invariably absent. In ready-made equipment the loudspeaker is often clamped in place by the circuit board, but this method does not lend itself well to many do-it-yourself projects, and looks like a rather dubious means of handling things anyway.

The normal way of dealing with the problem is to simply glue the loudspeaker in place, but first a cutout or grille of some kind is required, so that the sound from the loudspeaker has a reasonably clear route to the outside world. One way of tackling things is to make a circular cutout that is slightly smaller than the diameter of the loudspeaker. Some loudspeaker fret or material is then glued in place behind the cutout. The larger component catalogues usually list a few types of loudspeaker material, plus one or two types of loudspeaker fret.

Either fret or a material having a fairly fine pattern are the most suitable for use with miniature loudspeakers. Loudspeaker fret or material having a coarser pattern will work well enough, but may give the finished project a rather poor appearance. In the past expanded metal was popular for use as

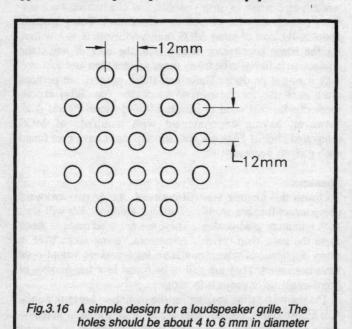

Fig.3.16 A simple design for a loudspeaker grille. The
         holes should be about 4 to 6 mm in diameter

loudspeaker fret, but this material seems to be relatively difficult to obtain these days. It is available from some craft shops, and might be obtainable from some of the larger do-it-yourself stores. A good quality general purpose adhesive is suitable for gluing loudspeaker material in place. Loudspeaker fret and expanded metal can be a bit more difficult to fix reliably, and a good gap filling adhesive such as an epoxy type is probably the best choice.

As an alternative to using some form of loudspeaker fret or material it is possible to simply drill the panel with a matrix of holes. I find that a matrix of five millimetre diameter holes, such as the design shown in Figure 3.16, gives good results. The sound from the loudspeaker is able to pass through the panel to the outside world, but the loudspeaker is given a reasonable amount of protection. This is an important point, since the diaphragm of the loudspeaker is very vulnerable to physical damage, and will probably be damaged before too long if it is not adequately protected.

The loudspeaker can be glued in place using a good quality general purpose adhesive, or an epoxy adhesive. Try not to smear any adhesive onto the diaphragm, especially if you use an epoxy adhesive. Adhesive on the diaphragm will not stop the loudspeaker from working, but it is almost certain to impair the audio quality.

Feeling the Squeeze

As I pointed out previously, fitting d.i.l. integrated circuits into their holders is often a little tricky. The reason for this is that, as supplied, the pins of d.i.l. integrated circuits are splayed outwards slightly, as in Figure 3.17(a). I am not entirely sure why the pins are formed into slightly the wrong shape, but it is probably to make it easier to implement automatic production systems. Unfortunately, it makes things a bit awkward for the home constructor.

It is much easier to fit integrated circuits into their holders if the two rows of pins are bent slightly inwards first (Figure 3.17(b). Simply squeezing the pins inwards with your fingers does not work well, particularly with larger devices. Using your fingers it is difficult to bend all the pins by the same amount, and the result is usually two rather wavy rows of pins which do

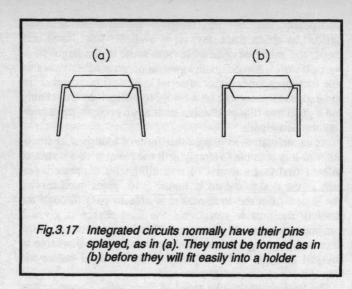

Fig.3.17 Integrated circuits normally have their pins splayed, as in (a). They must be formed as in (b) before they will fit easily into a holder

not fit into the holder very well. This gives a real risk of buckling one or more of the pins when inserting the device into its holder.

Probably the most common way of bending a row of pins is to hold them against flat a table-top, and then turn the body of the integrated circuit slightly in order to bend all the pins inwards by the same amount. There is actually a special tool for correctly forming integrated circuit pins, and this will operate with any normal size d.i.l. integrated circuit. All you have to do is drop the device into place, and then squeeze the tool firmly. Although I am not normally a proponent of clever devices such as this, I have to admit that this tool works extremely well, and is quite inexpensive as well.

Chapter 4

TROUBLESHOOTING AND FINISHING OFF

In an ideal world every project would work perfectly first time. In the real world a certain percentage of projects give a few problems, but with modern construction methods the percentage of problem projects should be quite small. If a high percentage of your projects fail to work first time, either you are extremely unlucky, or (more probably) you are being "slap-happy" when building the projects. More care when building the projects is the remedy, not improving your fault finding techniques!

As I have already pointed out more than once, prevention is better than cure. In most cases where a mistake is made, no damage will have been done. Correcting the mistake will result in the project firing on all four semiconductors. This can not be guaranteed though, and there is always a slight but real risk of mistakes causing damage to some of the components. Unfortunately, if any components are damaged as the result of an error, it is quite likely to be some of the semiconductors that come to grief. These are often the most expensive components in a project.

Therefore, as far as reasonably possible you should always endeavour to get things right first time. Being realistic about things, most of us are too impatient to give finished projects comprehensive checking prior to trying them out. However, you can carefully check things stage-by-stage during the construction process, so that the vast majority of errors are spotted and rectified before the project is finished. It is still a good idea to give the completed circuit board and wiring at least a cursory check before switching on a new project.

Mechanical Faults

Without some test equipment and the technical know-how to use it, the beginner can really only look for simple mechanical faults (accidental short circuits, "dry" joints, etc.). Fortunately, most faults in newly constructed equipment are of this type. The possibility of a faulty component can not be totally

117

discounted, but modern components are thoroughly tested and are incredibly reliable. I must have used hundreds of thousands of components over the years, but the number of "duds" I have encountered are extremely small.

At one time there was a problem with sub-standard transistors and diodes being remarked to make them look like the "real thing" so that they could be sold at full price. Fortunately, this practice of selling what were popularly known as "genuine duds" died out many years ago. Unless you have damaged a component while building a project, the chances of it failing to work due to a faulty component are probably many thousands to one against.

If, when you switch on a project for the first time, it is obviously malfunctioning, switch off at once to minimise the risk of damaging any of the components. If the circuit includes preset resistors it is as well to read the setting up instructions again to ensure that you have the right initial settings, and are correctly interpreting what is supposed to happen at switch-on.

The next step is to thoroughly check the circuit board and hard wiring. It is probably best to start with the hard wiring, as an error is more likely to occur here than on the circuit board. Check that the battery clip is connected the right way round, and that there are no crossed-over wires. Also check that each wire is properly connected at both ends. Particularly when using multi-way cables such as ribbon types, it is not always obvious if one wire is not connected properly, because the other wires may hold it roughly in the correct place.

Give the wires a good tug to check for poor soldered joints. Dry joints are often mechanically weak, and tugging on the wiring will often cause the lead to pull away from a bad joint. Look for excess semi-burnt flux around the joints, which is often to be found around poor joints. Also look for a dull or crazed surface on the blobs of solder. Again, this is often indicative of a poor quality joint. If in doubt, remove the solder from the joint, clean the end of the wire and the tag by scraping them with the small blade of a penknife, and then resolder the joint.

Are all the wires actually present? Missing out a lead is one of those errors that we all make eventually, and it is especially easy to make this mistake when eager to get your first projects complete. Count the number of wires on the wiring diagram and on your project to make sure that they tally correctly. Some constructors find it helpful to mark off each lead on the wiring diagram as it is added into the actual project.

Magnifying The Problem

If the wiring is all present and correct, turn your attention to the circuit board. Start by checking that all the components are in the correct positions, and the right way round. Check the resistor colour codes to ensure that you have used the right value for each component. The small size of modern resistors makes it difficult to read the colour codes on some of them. It is sometimes difficult to tell the difference between brown, red, and orange bands, particularly under artificial lighting. Using a magnifying glass usually makes it easier to correctly decipher colour codes, and also helps you to read values and type numbers correctly if they are written using tiny lettering.

One of the most common mistakes is to fit a component around the wrong way. Check all the polarised components, which usually means the electrolytic capacitors and (possibly) the diodes and rectifiers. The polarity markings on radial electrolytic capacitors are often quite small, and it might be worthwhile checking them using a magnifier.

Also check that the integrated circuits and (or) transistors are fitted correctly. Look carefully at the markings on the d.i.l. integrated circuits to ensure that you have not mistaken a moulding mark for the notch that indicates the pin 1 end of the case. With transistors it is easy to get the leadouts crossed over, or in some cases the device simply gets turned 90 degrees away from its correct orientation. Look carefully at the transistor leadout wires to ensure that there are no mistakes of these types. Also check the type numbers to ensure that each transistor is in the right place.

Solder Blobs

Accidental short circuits between adjacent copper strips are probably the most common problem when using stripboard. With the strips on a 0.1 inch pitch there has to be an extremely narrow gap between one copper strip and the next. In fact the gap is only about 0.5 millimetres. This means that only a small amount of excess solder is sufficient to produce a bridge of solder across two strips. Accidental short circuits are also quite common on custom printed circuit boards, which seem to become ever more intricate.

These unwanted short circuits across the strips can occur at any joint, but are most likely to occur where there are several closely spaced joints on different strips. This usually means areas of the board that are populated by d.i.l. integrated circuits. It is virtually inevitable that a number of accidental short circuits will be produced when using stripboard, but these will normally be spotted and corrected while you are building the board. The short circuits that cause the real problems are "the ones that get away."

Most of the offending solder blobs are visible to the naked eye if you look close enough. However, this is another example of a job that is much easier if a magnifying glass is used. Unless you have keen eyesight it is preferable to use a fairly powerful magnifier. I find that an 8× lupe (also known as a loupe) of the type used for examining photographic slides is ideal. A magnifier of this type should be available from your local photographic store.

Some solder blobs are not visible as they are hidden under flux, or other dirt on the board. Before making a visual inspection of the copper side of the board it is advisable to thoroughly clean it. Special cleaning fluids and sprays are available, but I find that vigourous brushing is effective at removing the flux and dirt. Something like an old nailbrush or toothbrush is suitable. With the board properly cleaned, a close visual inspection of the board will usually show up any solder blobs or trails, even if the problem is a minute trail of solder.

When making a visual check of the board try to be methodical, working across the board in a manner that does not leave any areas unchecked. As "Sod's" law dictates, if you miss out even a small piece of the board, that is where the problem will be located. The obvious method is to go along each pair of tracks from end to end, gradually working your way down the board. Past experience suggests that the problem is most likely to be in the vicinity of integrated circuits where the density of the soldered joints is quite high. Also, problems often seem to occur at the ends of the tracks. Solder trails at the very ends of boards can be difficult to spot, so look especially carefully at the ends of the tracks.

While making a detailed visual check of the board do not forget to check any breaks in the copper strips. Over the years I have had several projects that failed to work due to a copper track that was not completely cut. In each case the remaining copper was so thin that it was only visible with the aid of a magnifier.

Test Score

The most certain way of testing for short circuits between adjacent copper strips is to use a continuity tester. A continuity tester simply provides a visual or audible indication when there is a short circuit across the test prods. This is a popular type of project for beginners, and I would certainly recommend that you build or buy one of these at a fairly early stage. Some multi-range test meters ("multimeters") have this facility, or a multimeter set to a middle resistance range will do.

In this case the tests are made between adjacent copper strips, and continuity between the tracks (i.e. a short circuit) indicates that there is a problem. When using a continuity tester for this type of checking you must bear in mind that some testers are not very good at differentiating between a true short circuit and a low resistance. It is not just low resistances that give problems, and forward biased diode junctions can also produce false indications of continuity. These junctions are not just present in diodes, but are to be found in transistors, integrated circuits, and other semiconductors. In fact the average circuit board is liberally sprinkled with these hidden diode junctions.

Unless you have a discriminating continuity tester that can ignore diode junctions there is probably no point in using it to check for short circuits on stripboards. There should be no problem if you use a multimeter set to a resistance range, as it will indicate a low but significant resistance if it is connected across a diode junction. A multimeter should also be able to differentiate between a resistance of a few ohms or more and a true short circuit.

You may occasionally find that the continuity tester indicates that there is a short circuit, but a visual check reveals nothing. You should first ensure that there is no link-wire providing an intentional short circuit across the two copper strips in question. If there is no intended short circuit and you can not see the offending piece of solder, try scoring between the pair of strips using a modelling knife. If this is repeated a few times it should clear any small pieces of solder between the tracks, or reveal any larger pieces that are hidden under flux or dirt.

Some years ago when I was building quite large numbers of projects using stripboard, when a new project failed to work I would, as a matter of course, use this scoring process between all the copper tracks. In a surprisingly large percentage of cases this brought the project to life. If all else fails, it is certainly worth giving it a try. Obviously due care must be taken whenever using a sharp knife, and this is no exception. A fair amount of pressure should be exerted on the knife, but the slightly brittle nature of some stripboards must be taken into account. Use a large amount of pressure and the board will almost certainly break.

Damaged Components

Although they are mostly very small, modern electronic components are mostly quite tough. However, this is not to say that they are indestructible, and it is possible to damage components when fitting them to the board. The obvious risk is that of overheating components when soldering them in place. Provided your solder technique is up to a reasonable standard this should rarely (if ever) happen.

Apart from vulnerable components such as germanium diodes, damage due to overheating will usually produce some outward sign of the problem. In most cases this means a darkening in the body colour, possibly with the paint or outer skin of the component peeling off to some extent. If there is any obvious damage of this type and you have no way of testing the component, it is probably best to replace it, especially in the case of inexpensive components such as resistors and small capacitors.

In my experience, the components that are most vulnerable to physical damage are printed circuit mounting capacitors of the uncased variety. The lack of an outer casing makes it relatively easy to pull off one of the leadout wires. Early capacitors of this type were notorious for losing a leadout wire when they were being fitted onto the circuit board. Only very slight outward force was needed on the leadout wires in order to rip them away from the body of the component.

Modern uncased capacitors seem to be somewhat tougher, but there can still be occasional problems with leadout wires pulling away. This type of capacitor should only be used on circuit boards which have the correct lead spacing. Trying to form the leads in order to make them fit into a different spacing often results in one of the leadout wires becoming detached. Sometimes a capacitor of this type seems to have been fitted in place all right, but close inspection reveals that one of the leadouts has become detached. The lead is soldered in place, but is not quite in contact with the body of the capacitor.

If careful checking of the board fails to reveal any errors, simply pulling firmly on each component, one-by-one, may reveal a detached lead, a bad joint, or even a lead which you have forgotten to solder in place. Particularly with stripboard, an omitted connection can be difficult to spot, and it is an error most of us make from time to time. The usual cause is that you have soldered one lead of a component in place, and have then had to stop to (say) answer the telephone. On returning you then fail to notice that the second lead has been trimmed but not soldered in place. Where possible, finish the task you are currently undertaking before stopping work on a circuit board.

Buckling Under

Take a close look at the d.i.l. integrated circuits to ensure that they are all in their holders correctly. If you do not get the integrated circuits fully pushed into their holders, they may tend to spring back out again. Are both rows of pins inserted into the holder properly? With some types of holder it is possible to have devices which appear to be plugged in correctly, but when you look closely it is apparent that only one row of pins is actually in place.

The problem could be that one or two of the pins buckled as they were pushed into their holders. If a pin buckles outwards it is usually fairly obvious, but is something that you might have missed if you were not looking closely when fitting the integrated circuits. It might be worthwhile removing the integrated circuits from their holders to check the pins. If a pin buckles inwards it can be difficult to spot while the device is still in its socket. In fact a buckled pin can go through practically 180 degrees, making it very difficult to spot unless the integrated circuit is removed from its holder.

It is possible to buy tools for removing integrated circuits from their holders, but in most cases it is quite easy to prise them free using the blade of a small screwdriver to release one end and then the other. Do not try to remove an integrated circuit using your fingers. This almost invariably results in one end of the device pulling well clear of the holder while the other end is still in place. This in turn results in some of the pins being bent right out of position, or even snapped off.

If an integrated circuit pin should become buckled it is usually possible to carefully straighten it out again. Try to get the pin as straight as possible. Putting the blade of a screwdriver behind the pin and then pressing it firmly against the blade with a fingernail usually straightens the pin very well. If a pin is left slightly kinked it is quite likely that it will buckle again when the device is replaced in its holder.

If a pin should break off, it may be possible to rescue the device provided there is still at least a small piece of the pin protruding from the body of the component. A small piece of wire must be used as a substitute for the missing part of the pin. Solder about 40 millimetres of 22 s.w.g. tinned copper wire to what is left of the pin. Then trim the wire to the same length as the remaining pins, and bend the surrogate pin into position. It should then be possible to carefully manoeuvre the integrated circuit into its holder, and the piece of wire should make good contact with the holder.

Second Opinion

If a thorough check of the circuit board and wiring fails to cure the fault, ideally you should get someone else to check the project for you. It could well be that there is a glaring mistake, but having fooled yourself into making the mistake in the first place, it is all too easy to go on fooling yourself thereafter. A fresh pair of eyes looking at the project will probably not be fooled in the same way, and will quickly spot the cause of the problem.

Obviously many constructors will not have someone with the necessary knowledge to check the project for them, although anyone who is reasonably intelligent should be able to check the construction diagrams against your unit. If no helper can be found, the next best thing is to put the project aside for a week or two, and then take a fresh look at it. In the intervening week or so you will become less familiar with the project, and will be able to look at it more objectively.

Skin Deep

While it has to be admitted that making a project "look pretty" will not improve its performance, I think it is fair to say that most of us would prefer to produce neat looking projects rather than complete eyesores. It is perhaps worth making the point that no matter how much craftsmanship has gone into the interior of a project, most people will judge it by its exterior finish. Even if you are not particularly keen on this aspect of electronic project construction, it is probably worthwhile putting a little money and effort into making completed projects look good.

Using a stylish and well made case will help to produce a first rate finished product, but it is a case of "you get what you pay for." Top quality cases tend to cost relatively large amounts, and it is not unusual for a top quality case to cost several times as much as a simple case having similar dimensions. For most of us there is no alternative to using an inexpensive case and making it look as good as possible.

Up to Scratch

The most inexpensive of cases are plastic boxes and simple folded aluminium boxes. Slightly further up the price scale there are instrument cases which have an aluminium base, front, and rear panel, plus a steel outer casing, or a steel outer casing with aluminium front and rear panels. A common problem with many of these cases is that, at no extra charge, they come complete with a few minor scratches, moulding marks, etc. In order to obtain a neat finish these must be either removed or covered.

Provided the scratches or other marks are just superficial, it should be possible to polish them out using practically any metal polish ("Duraglit", "Brasso", or anything similar). This method works equally well with plastic and metal cases. It is actually quite possible to polish out more severe scratches on plastic cases, but this can be quite time consuming, and is not necessarily worth the effort.

Finding a "needle in a haystack" is difficult, but it is more difficult to find a needle in a stack of needles. This philosophy can be applied to front panel scratches by hiding them in a multitude of tiny scratches. These scratches can be made by rubbing the panel with a fairly coarse grade of wire-wool (or a small piece of "Brillo-Pad"). This process does not work well with most plastic cases, but it should give good results with aluminium types.

It is possible to produce some quite fancy patterns with crisscrossed lines and so on, but if you are going to try this sort of thing it is best to experiment first on some scrap pieces of aluminium. Progress to a real case only when you have mastered the patterning process. If you want to keep things simple, just use parallel scratches along the full length of the front panel. The panel may look a little rough once the treatment has been completed, but it can be polished using a soft cloth. This should leave quite a good "brushed aluminium" effect finish.

If an aluminium panel has a scratch-free finish it can be polished to a shiny and attractive finish using a soft cloth. The problem with aluminium panels that once polished to a good finish they soon seem to oxidise, and also retain finger marks. What starts out as an attractive finish can soon deteriorate to a dull and dirty appearance. Panels that are given the "brushed aluminium" look seem to be even more vulnerable to this problem than plain aluminium panels. The problem is easily solved, and it is just a matter of spraying aluminium panels with a transparent lacquer.

Cover-Up

The obvious way of dealing with scratches and other marks is to cover them up with a few coats of paint. However, experience has shown that quite minor scratches will often show quite clearly through several coats of paint. Another problem with painting cases is that it can be difficult to get the paint to adhere properly to aluminium and some of the plastics that are commonly used for inexpensive cases. Some paints adhere very well to most plastic cases (particularly quick drying types), but they seem to etch their way into the surface of the case. This can give some odd effects, with gloss paints that produce a rather dull finish for example. You can also end up with some rather odd colours! I generally avoid painting cases as the results are often far from perfect, and things are generally unpredictable.

The more reliable method of covering scratches is to use some form of veneer. Even if a panel has a scratch-free finish, using a veneer of some kind might produce a much more attractive finish. Although there are numerous self-adhesive plastic veneers available, many of these are not really a great deal of use in the current context. Most are heavily patterned and are great for covering shelves, etc., but are totally inappropriate for the front panels of electronic projects. If you can find a plain self-adhesive plastic material in a suitable colour this should do the job well.

Various leather grain effect plastic veneers are available, but these are again not well suited to the front panels of electronic projects. They are mainly intended for covering outer casings, speaker cabinets, and the like. However, they might be apposite for certain types of project. These veneers are not normally of the self-adhesive variety incidentally, but are easily glued in place using a good quality general purpose adhesive.

The best front panel veneer that I have found so far is a brushed aluminium effect type that is available from some of the larger component retailers. I think that I am correct in stating that this is a plastic veneer which does not contain any aluminium at all, but it certainly does an excellent imitation of the "real thing". It also provides an extremely hard-wearing finish. There is a major problem with many plastic veneers in that they tend to deteriorate and become very brittle after a couple of years. So far, I have not encountered any problems with this veneer deteriorating in any way, even after many years.

This brushed aluminium effect veneer is very much thicker than most self-adhesive veneers, and it is actually quite rigid. The best way to cut it is using a sharp modelling knife and a metal ruler or plastic ruler having a metal insert for cutting purposes. The adhesive is very powerful, and will reliably stick the veneer to aluminium and plastic front panels. In fact the strength of the adhesive is such that it can be difficult to remove the veneer and reposition it, so if possible, get it right first time. On the plus side, as this material is quite rigid, it is easier to deal with than are most self-adhesive materials. There is little risk of it folding over and sticking to itself for example.

Covering the front panel of a plastic case with a veneer can be a bit awkward due to the rounded corners that are found on many these cases. I find that the best approach is to cut the veneer to the correct size but with "square" corners, and to trim the corners once the veneer has been fixed to the front panel. Even one of the tougher veneers, such as the brushed aluminum effect veneer, can be trimmed using a good pair of scissors.

To the Letter

Practically any project can be made to look much more professional if the controls and sockets are given neat labels. In fact this is not just a matter of making projects look prettier, and good labelling will make the projects easier to use. Labelling everything is especially important with larger projects that are bristling with controls and sockets. Without proper labelling, using a project of this type becomes a matter of guesswork until you become really accustomed to using it.

If you are really not interested in this aspect of construction, which can be surprisingly time consuming, a simple labelling machine is probably the best option. There are actually some labelling machines that are capable of producing top quality results, but these have prices which put them well beyond the means of most home constructors. Here we are concerned with the low cost devices that can be obtained from many stationers, such as the "Dymo" labellers. One of these costs only a few pounds, and is supplied complete with at least one self-adhesive tape. A single tape will probably be sufficient to provide the labels for dozens of projects, making this one of the cheapest methods of producing panel legends.

To produce a label you simply dial up each letter in turn, pressing the button on the side of the device after each selection. Pressing the button transfers the selected letter onto the tape and advances the tape. Producing each label usually takes less than a minute, and a full set of labels for a major project can be produced in ten minutes or so. Labelling machines are almost certainly the quickest means of producing worthwhile panel labels. The self-adhesive labels are easily fitted to projects, but reasonable care should be taken over their positioning. Try to get them properly centred above the controls and sockets, and avoid any obvious slanting.

Although this method offers a very quick, cheap, and easy means of producing panel labels, it does have a couple of drawbacks. One is simply that the labels are not particularly small, and it can be difficult to accommodate them properly on some miniature projects. Most projects have sufficient panel space for them though. The second problem is simply that the labels produced are relatively crude, and do not give the professional looking results that are possible with some other methods of lettering. However, if you do not wish to spend much time or money on panel legends, this method is almost certainly the best option.

The Rub

Rub-on transfers are the main alternative to self-adhesive labels. A vast range of letter sizes and styles are available, and any stationery shop should be able to offer a good selection. In general, lettering about three to four millimetres high is most suitable for labelling the controls of projects. For miniature projects it might be necessary to use smaller lettering having a height of 2.5 or even two millimetres. For most projects a fairly conservative lettering style (font) is the most appropriate. It can be useful to have some larger letters, say about six to eight millimetres high, if you wish to add names on projects (e.g. "Microphone Compressor" or "Three Band Radio"). You might also prefer to use a fancier font for this sort of thing, particularly for projects of a non-serious nature such as electronic games.

With self-adhesive labels there is usually no difficulty in finishing the project first, and then adding the labels. This is not a practical proposition with rub-on transfers, which can only be applied to a panel if it is free from obstructions such as control knobs, and the controls themselves. Either the labels must be added once all the drilling has been completed (but before final assembly of the unit), or the completed and tested project must be partially dismantled so that the labels can be added.

When using self-adhesive labels I have never found it necessary to use any form of guide to help with accurate positioning. Provided due care is taken, results are perfectly acceptable with the labels positioned "by eye". The same is not true when using rub-on transfers, which require much more trouble and care if neat results are to be obtained. It is usually more than a little helpful if some guide marks are added to the panel, to help keep the lettering on one level and slant-free. Lengths of tape across the full width of the panel are my preferred method of marking guide lines. An alternative is to mark the lines on the front panel using a fibre-tipped pen having a spirit based ink, but with this method it might be impossible to remove the lines without damaging the lettering.

I find that a brightly coloured insulation tape is the best way of providing guide lines. The tape must be stretched quite tightly to ensure that it is straight enough, and care must be taken to ensure that it is not positioned at a slight angle. It will be necessary to add two or three small guide marks to the panel before fitting the tape. If the lettering is to be on more than one level, add the top level first, and work your way down the panel. Most transfer sheets have guide marks for use with guide lines on the work-piece, and the tape must obviously be positioned such that the lettering has the correct vertical placement when these guide marks are used.

Self-Centred

Some careful planning is needed before starting each label. The main problem is in getting the words correctly centred above the controls and sockets. Adding centre marks on the guide tapes helps, but you then have to accurately guesstimate the centre of each word. As an example, the centre of the word "volume" would seem to be between the third and fourth letters, as there are six letters in the word. On the face of it, the label will be accurately centred if the "l" and the "u" are placed either side of the centre mark, and the other letters added, working outwards from these.

This method will work quite well, but there is a slight catch in that the letter "l" is narrower than the other letters. This shifts the centre point towards the "u", a factor which must be taken into account if the label is to be centred really accurately. If you only use upper case letters for labels there will probably be less of a problem in centring the labels, as there is less variation in the width of upper case letters. The letter "I" is the main one to watch out for.

Many transfer sheets have guide marks which are intended to aid the correct spacing from one letter to the next. Most of these systems allow for the fact that the letters are not all the same width, and provide more or less space for each letter, as appropriate. This is known as proportional spacing incidentally. I would advise against relying too heavily on these guide systems. Most people can produce neater results if the letters are positioned "by eye", as you can then provide what is known as kerning.

When letters such as "A" and "W" are used side-by-side, proportional spacing gives what tends to be perceived as an excessive gap between the letters. Kerning is the process of moving letters closer together or further apart so that the apparent gap between them is the same, and neat results are obtained. In the case of the letters "A" and "W", their complementary shapes make it necessary to move them closer together in order to obtain what is perceived as normal spacing. This is another factor which can shift the centre of a label, although in most cases its effect is too small to be of any practical significance.

Rub-on transfers seem to adhere well to practically any plastic case, and also to metal panels. I find that results are best if only a moderate amount of pressure is used during the rub-on process. I also find that results are better using the proper spatula tool rather than an old pencil or ball-point pen. Try not to lean heavily on the sheet, or you may well find that you have inadvertently added odd bits of lettering all over the panel!

By combining the two ideas it is possible to have much of the convenience of self-adhesive labels, together with the neat appearance of rub-on transfers. Transparent self-adhesive material is available from most stationers, and makes a good basis for labels. Simply put the required words onto the self-adhesive material, cut them out, peel off the backing material, and stick them in place on the panel. The backing material is transparent rather than invisible, and consequently this method gives slightly less professional results than applying the transfers direct to the panel. However, it is a quite quick and easy means of obtaining a good overall standard of finish.

Brush Off

Although rub-on transfers can provide some really professional results, they often look rather scrappy after a project has been in use for a few weeks. The problem is that they rub off almost as easily as they rub on! I would recommend providing some form of protection for rub-on transfers, or a lot of hard work will soon be ruined.

The easiest way of protecting them is to use some form of transparent lacquer, and a spray type is the best choice. Some of these lacquers have the potential to dissolve the lettering, and applying one of these by brush is likely to produce a front panel that will resemble a piece of modern art. There is little risk of the lettering "running" if a spray-on lacquer or fixative is used in accordance with the manufacturer's recommendations. In particular, do not apply too much in one coat. Aerosol cans of transparent lacquer and fixative are available from the larger stationers, and from practically any art materials shop.

A few coats of a lacquer or fixative give a reasonable amount of protection to the transfers, but they can still be accidentally scratched off by fingernails or any generally rough treatment. I have only found one way of making them genuinely scratch resistant, and that is to cover them with some transparent self-adhesive material.

On the face of it this is easy enough, but there is a potential snag. If you do not lay down the covering perfectly first time, peeling it back and trying again will almost certainly result in some of the lettering coming away on the plastic covering. Therefore, if you use this method, strive to get everything right first time, and be prepared to start from scratch if things go wrong. Life will be much easier if you can find one of the thicker grades of the material. These seem to be much easier to manoeuvre into position, with less tendency to produce wrinkles and air bubbles. Small air bubbles can be removed by bursting then with a pin, and then pressing the material down into place.

Hi-Tech

If you have access to a computer and a good quality printer you might like to try using this to make panel labels. In order to make simple labels you do not need any particularly advanced software, and these days most word processors and d.t.p. programs provide you with at least a few lettering styles which can be printed in a wide range of sizes. Many of these programs offer proportional spacing or even kerning.

Computer aided drawing (CAD) and illustration programs also offer a wide range of text sizes in a variety of fonts. The advantage of a CAD or illustration program is that it is possible to print out designs accurately to scale. This opens up the possibility of producing complete front panel designs (Figure 4.1) rather than just producing individual labels. It is possible to produce some excellent and highly professional looking front panels using this method.

Once you have learned to use the software, it is possible to produce completed front panels surprisingly quickly. It is not worthwhile obtaining a computer system specifically to produce your own front panels, but if you already have a suitable computer system it might be worthwhile seeking out a low cost CAD or illustration program. For IBM PCs and compatible there are some public domain and shareware programs that would probably be worth investigating.

For the best results use a fairly thick and high quality paper. Remember that you are not restricted to an inverse Ford choice (any colour you like provided it is white), and coloured papers can provide some attractive results. The paper overlay can be fixed to the front panel using any general purpose adhesive, or a simple paste will usually do the job quite well. Use the smallest amount of adhesive that will do the job properly, or the glue may leak through to the front side of the paper. Double-sided tape provides another means of fixing the overlays, and this avoids any possibility of the adhesive leaking through to the front side of the overlay.

Most printers produce an overlay that is quite resistant to scratching, but the paper may soon start to discolour or become dirty. Coating the panel with fixative or transparent lacquer might give a better finish and a more durable front panel, but there can be unwanted side-effects, such as the overlay going

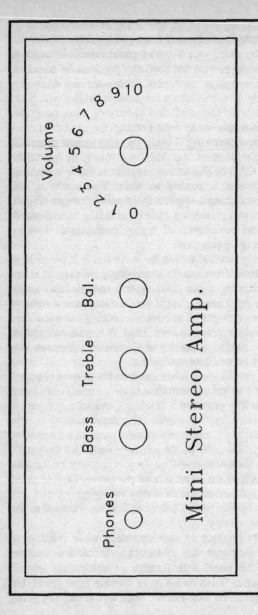

Fig.4.1   An example front panel overlay produced using a CAD program

Phones   Bass   Treble   Bal.

Mini Stereo Amp.

Volume

0 1 2 3 4 5 6 7 8 9 10

134

translucent! Covering the panel with transparent self-adhesive plastic is the better choice. Apart from giving plenty of protection to the overlay, it also gives a very professional looking finish. It there should be problems when covering the panel, it does not take long to print out a new overlay and try again.

And Finally . . .
Newcomers to practically any hobby seem to be experts at convincing themselves that it is all too difficult, and that they will never be able to do it. Electronic project construction probably suffers from this syndrome more than most hobbies, but it is really not that difficult to build a few simple projects. You will have some new skills to acquire, and there will be some challenges along the way, but it would be a boring waste of time if there was no challenge and it was "as easy as a, b, c."

It is tempting to start by building a complex project that has some weird and wonderful function, but unless you are exceptionally talented this is definitely a mistake. The bigger the project, the greater the scope for making mistakes. Also, some beginners build complex projects and have problems simply because they do not really understand its exact function. Start with a simple project that does something fairly straightforward (a household gadget or a simple care project for example). There are bound to be a few points that you do not understand initially, but when you get started on your first project you will find that things start to fall into place. Having constructed your first project you will probably be "hooked for life."

Hot Like Fire
and Other Poems